Cambridge Elements

Elements in Christian Doctrine
edited by
Rachel Muers
University of Edinburgh
Ashley Cocksworth
University of Roehampton
Simeon Zahl
University of Cambridge

A THEOLOGY OF BECOMING

Body, Blood, Birth, and Sacrament

Tina Beattie
University of Roehampton

Shaftesbury Road, Cambridge CB2 8EA, United Kingdom

One Liberty Plaza, 20th Floor, New York, NY 10006, USA

477 Williamstown Road, Port Melbourne, VIC 3207, Australia

314–321, 3rd Floor, Plot 3, Splendor Forum, Jasola District Centre, New Delhi – 110025, India

103 Penang Road, #05–06/07, Visioncrest Commercial, Singapore 238467

Cambridge University Press is part of Cambridge University Press & Assessment, a department of the University of Cambridge.

We share the University's mission to contribute to society through the pursuit of education, learning and research at the highest international levels of excellence.

www.cambridge.org
Information on this title: www.cambridge.org/9781009535540

DOI: 10.1017/9781009535571

© Tina Beattie 2026

This publication is in copyright. Subject to statutory exception and to the provisions of relevant collective licensing agreements, no reproduction of any part may take place without the written permission of Cambridge University Press & Assessment.

When citing this work, please include a reference to the DOI 10.1017/9781009535571

First published 2026

A catalogue record for this publication is available from the British Library

ISBN 978-1-009-53554-0 Hardback
ISBN 978-1-009-53556-4 Paperback
ISSN 2977-0211 (online)
ISSN 2977-0203 (print)

Cambridge University Press & Assessment has no responsibility for the persistence or accuracy of URLs for external or third-party internet websites referred to in this publication and does not guarantee that any content on such websites is, or will remain, accurate or appropriate.

For EU product safety concerns, contact us at Calle de José Abascal, 56, 1°, 28003 Madrid, Spain, or email eugpsr@cambridge.org

A Theology of Becoming

Body, Blood, Birth, and Sacrament

Elements in Christian Doctrine

DOI: 10.1017/9781009535571
First published online: January 2026

Tina Beattie
University of Roehampton
Author for correspondence: Tina Beattie, tina@tinabeattie.com

Abstract: Modern theological approaches to birth have been filtered through an androcentric lens, focusing more on ethical questions of contraception and abortion than on the significance of birth for what it means to be human. In the Catholic tradition, this has been influenced by doctrines and traditions surrounding Mary's virginal conception of Christ and painless birth. This Element considers the challenges posed by maternal life to ideas and theories about pregnancy, childbirth, and the relationship between a woman and her newborn child. Reflecting on her maternal experiences through the lenses of feminist theory and Marian theology, the author sketches the contours of an incarnational theology that endows the birthing body with sacramental significance. She concludes by asking what it would mean for theological anthropology to adopt this as the normative model of the person reborn through baptism into the body of the maternal Church.

This Element also has a video abstract:
www.cambridge.org/ECDR_Beattie_abstract

Keywords: childbirth, matrescence, feminism, theology, sacramentality

© Tina Beattie 2026

ISBNs: 9781009535540 (HB), 9781009535564 (PB), 9781009535571 (OC)
ISSNs: 2977-0211 (online), 2977-0203 (print)

Contents

	Introduction	1
	PART I: PRECONCEPTIONS	2
1	How to Begin?	2
	PART II: CONCEPTIONS	13
2	Body	13
3	Blood	27
4	Birth	40
5	Sacrament	49
6	Redeeming Birth	61
	References	66

A Theology of Becoming

Introduction

This Element emerged from a seminar paper I presented in 2015 at the Yale Center for Faith and Culture. Professor Miroslav Volf invited me to contribute to a consultation on Birth, as part of the 'God and Human Flourishing' project at Yale. Other contributors to the consultation were Dr James Mumford, Revd Dr Michael Banner, and Professor Lisa Guenther.

Mumford's book, *Ethics at the Beginning of Life: A Phenomenological Critique*, gave me a steer in the direction of my contribution to the seminar. He writes:

> For phenomenology, the 'I' who is the 'absolute source' of perception is no detached consciousness but rather 'defined by (its) situation' and thoroughly rooted in the world. Accordingly, any description of human emergence must be committed to describing the phenomenon from the perspective of the mother – as Luce Irigaray puts it, 'She who has been the company and the mediator of our first being in the world'. (Mumford, 2013: xii, quoting Merleau-Ponty, 1962: vii and Irigaray, 2008: 117)

I decided I would write my paper as a dialogue with Mumford. I was the mother of four adult children and a Catholic theologian researching issues of gender, sexuality, and sacramentality, employing an Irigarayan approach to language. I had spent twenty years studying that most potent and sublime representation of motherhood – the Virgin Mary, Mother of God. Admittedly, she had a somewhat unusual experience of conception and birth, if we are to believe what we are told, but I shall come to that.

Mumford's phenomenology of birth, however, turned out to be the prolegomenon to an ethical argument against abortion, and that was not the topic I wanted to focus on. I had written extensively on abortion (e.g., Beattie, 2009 and 2014), but could I attempt something more radical and personal by bringing my own maternal life into a phenomenological perspective?

I wrote what I believed was lacking from Mumford's book, reaching back through time to drag my young birthing, bleeding, lactating body into language. This meant enfleshing the spectral presence of the maternal subject, who fades away as Mumford's argument against abortion develops, by changing the focus from a male author seeking to interpret the maternal voice to a maternal author seeking her own voice.

While this Element is indebted to that Yale seminar for its original stimulus, it is not intended as a critical analysis of any particular scholar's work. Rather, I am concerned with what is at stake with regard to mainstream theology's failure to take seriously the challenges posed by the emergence of women's voices out of domesticated silence into theological speech. The narratives of birth I introduce to theological discourse are intended to expose the assumptions of androcentric authority and mastery that still pervade the Christian intellectual tradition in Western scholarship. Women's voices are domesticated, appropriated, interrupted, and interpreted in such a way that the theological edifice is reinforced rather than undermined, its moral judgements legitimised, and its interpretative authority affirmed.

A theological account of birth developed through a maternal phenomenology would be a bloody rupture in the theological corpus, entailing a confrontation with the primal howl of origins, by way of which even the most esteemed professor, pope, or bishop was pushed into life through a woman's vagina, covered in her slime, shit, and blood. *Inter faeces et urinem nascimur* – we are born between shit and piss, goes a saying attributed to Augustine and Bernard of Clairvaux. (Early and medieval theologians, mystics, and artists were less squeamish than their modern counterparts about these bodily realities, perhaps because neither birth nor death was hidden from sight in the sanitised artifice of a hospital ward.) To conceive of these beginnings would effect a conceptual revolution by bringing into language the acts of conception and birth that are the origins of every human life and of the Christian story, in which even God has a Mother.

PART I: PRECONCEPTIONS

1 How to Begin?

I love you. I want you. I hate you. I rape you.

How do we know what whispered intimacies of tenderness or threats of violence seeded us in our mothers' wombs?

One does not need to make love to make a child. Rape will do just as well. Either way, that momentary ejaculation for a man has life-changing consequences for the woman who discovers she is pregnant, whatever the outcome. As the zygote begins to grow, an exchange of cells between the maternal and foetal bodies will leave a physical trace of the other's presence – a little-understood and under-researched phenomenon known as microchimerism (Thomasy, 2024; Wu, 2024).

A woman might have an early miscarriage before she knows she's pregnant, in which case, the trace of an unformed presence will remain in her DNA but not in her memory or her heart. She might miscarry later in the pregnancy, decide to end the pregnancy, experience a stillbirth, or die in childbirth. But if she is a white middle-class woman with access to good obstetric care, chances are that she and her infant will survive if she decides to continue with the pregnancy. They will survive, but she will never be the same again.

I know the violence and humiliation of sex without love, but my four children were conceived in love. We have been making love for more than fifty years, and we're not finished yet. The making of love is a lifelong discipline of struggle and rest, yearning and delight, satisfaction and frustration, which has less and less to do with sex and more and more to do with wondering, what is this thing called love that we are making? It is a task that must remain unfinished, for there is always a remainder, a yearning for love that no human relationship can satisfy. This is the fathomless longing of eros without an object that mystics recognise as the soul's panting for God (Kamitsuka, 2024a), and psychoanalysts associate with the vanquished presence of the pre-oedipal mother.

This Element is not about mysticism and erotic passion, nor about marriage and the domestication of desire. It is not about making babies, which takes two, with one unique exception. Unlike my academic monographs, it mentions psychoanalytic theory only in passing.

It is about what happens to a woman after the conceptual event. No matter how much love is being made between them, no matter how faithful and committed the father might be, this is an experience that he can only observe as a vicarious outsider. He has the option to walk away or stay, but she carries the consequences of the act within her own body. As James Mumford points out: 'the newone is closer to the mother than anyone could possibly be; the baby, unlike the penis of her lover, a woman harbours whole' (2013: 19).

Mumford asks, 'What has befallen the way we define, value, construe, and account for encounters between human beings in general, and how does that affect how we compute the mother's experience?' (2013: 30). How do we conceptualise conception? That is the question. But who are 'we', and where should 'we' begin – with books or births?

'In the beginning was the Word' (John 1:1). We are born into a world that was worded into being, into texts already written, words already spoken, linguistic maps that will mark out the borders and horizons of our gendered becoming. Concepts come before conceptions. St Augustine tells us that the Virgin Mary conceived Christ first in her mind and then in her womb – *prius mente quam ventre concipens* (Augustine, *Sermo* 215). The English translation misses the poetic playfulness of the Latin, and our language should be playfully poetic when we speak of such intimacies.

Jacques Derrida claims that, contra Jean-Jacques Rousseau, reading and writing constitute a more immediate and accessible, self-deconstructing presence than the absence they mask, the 'dangerous supplement' of the mother/nature for which language is an inadequate substitute: 'If, premeditating the theme of writing, I began by speaking of the substitution of mothers, it is because, as Rousseau will himself say, "more depends on this than you realize"' (Derrida, 1976: 146. See also Chapter 5 of Battersby, 1998).

Yes, indeed. So let us set aside the maternal body, that dangerous supplement/*différance* that lures us into fantasies of plenitude, seducing us to grope through the gaps in language to encounter only absence and lack: 'Nature, that which words like "real mother" name, have always already escaped, have never existed; that which opens meaning and language is writing as the disappearance of natural presence' (Derrida, 1976: 159). We begin where we find ourselves, in texts that are a poor substitute for that vanished/vanquished (m)other: 'We must begin *wherever we are* and the thought of the trace, which cannot take the scent into account, has already taught us that it was impossible to justify a point of departure absolutely. *Wherever we are*: in a text where we already believe ourselves to be' (Derrida, 1976: 162).

Mother and child bear the elusive microchimera of the other within their DNA, as language bears the elusive trace of the mother within its structure, but how do we sniff her out? How do we hear the cries of orgasm or terror by which we were conceived? How do we smell the blood and water that gushed us into the light? How do we feel the naked breast against our cheek and taste its milky consolations? The 'I' is the eviscerated bodily self, written and rewritten, represented and replicated in texts upon texts, veiling the womb/tomb of our origins and endings with words that hold the abyss at bay.

Wending her way through twentieth-century texts of psychoanalytic and literary theory, nature/mother is a phantasm, a ghostly apparition evoked by writing as a lingering trace of that which is experienced as lack. For Derrida, this is the whimsical and elusive feminine/woman hovering on the edges of meaning, resisting any attempt at definition or fixity. For Lacan, it is the unattainable Mother/God for whom the infant soul yearns with the white fire of unwritten, unspoken desire beyond all desires. The term 'white fire' comes from the Talmud: 'When the Talmud says that the Torah given to Moses was written "in black fire on white fire," it ... emphasizes the distinction between the language of the Torah, which exists eternally (or, as we now say, virtually), and its physical medium' (Kirsch, 2018). Our identities are stories written in black ink on the white fire of a haunting and mysterious otherness.

So I begin with books and texts, but my purpose is to write (as) the maternal body, to scavenge among the discarded remnants of language and rehabilitate them in writing differently, in writing *différance* by allowing language to be unsettled through the articulation of bodiliness, desire, and desolation. This means allowing imagined memories to disrupt the settled meaning and the conclusive argument. This task finds expression in Cixous's concept of *écriture féminine* (Cixous, 1976) and Kristeva's articulation of love and abjection as the hauntings of otherness that fracture the cohesion of the symbolic subject (Kristeva, 1982 and 1987).

That is the direction in which I am moving, but for now, I set aside the mother and God, the dangerous supplement(s) that leak into language, just as blood and milk sometimes leak through the laundered surfaces of a woman's clothes. I shall begin with books, keeping my womb words warm as I introduce the ideas that seeded this text, this wild, unruly child of an academic encounter. Speaking with a forked tongue, weaving a story on the loom of my two selves, I write as an academic and a mother. I create a doubled persona who is mind and matter/mater, conceptualising and conceiving, labouring over texts to rebirth an ancient story told by men.

> Woman must write her self: must write about women and bring women to writing, from which they have been driven away as violently as from their bodies – for the same reasons, by the same law, with the same fatal goal. Woman must put herself into the text – as into the world and into history – by her own movement. (Cixous, 1976: 875)

1.1 Conceptual Beginnings

In developing that original seminar paper for a wider audience, I have had to overcome my resistance to the appeal to experience, which forms the methodological foundation for liberal feminist theologies. By the time I attended university as a mature student and discovered feminist theological writings, I was a mother of four children, with a nomadic soul shaped by a diasporic Scottish colonial and postcolonial African upbringing. I had struggled with an existential yearning for God from the Presbyterian Church of my childhood through various experiments with agnosticism, atheism, Anglicanism, and evangelicalism, before finally converting to Catholicism – not because it provided answers, but because it helped me to understand my questions. It located me within a continuing story of humankind's failed endeavours to overcome the violent and destructive tendencies of our species with an ethos of active love for the most abjected and despised of our neighbours in need. Discovering the Catholic tradition was an invitation to contemplate the divine mystery in art and music, architecture and ritual, draping my inarticulate prayers in liturgical rhythms and seasons softened by incense and candlelight. Through it all, a vast maternal presence enveloped me, overcoming the resistance and suspicions of my Protestant upbringing. The Mother of God became an all-pervasive presence in my life.

This personal history makes me aware of the layers of social conditioning, false consciousness, and psychological turbulence through which we navigate a path of meaning throughout life, inscribing our bodies in language that is never enough. There is always a remainder, a pulsing, fleshy, animal self which grunts and groans and sings and squawks its presence. There are memories that will not be contained, desires that will not be controlled, terrors that will not be tamed, and dreams that will not be foreclosed. Random events take hold of us and shake us up, rearranging our stories, taking root in our bodies, and demanding that we ask again and again who we are and where we belong as mortal, vulnerable creatures in a creation suffused with the majesty, mystery, and dread of the Creator.

Mindful of all this, my brief late-life academic career did not rely on the unreliable guide of experience, but wandered through sacramental theology, Lacanian psycholinguistics, and feminist theory, in a quest that sought fidelity to the truthful chaos of female bodily life, without exposing too much of myself. Theology and theory provided linguistic veils that spared my blushes and protected my sense that experience was not to be trusted, and I was no body worth speaking of. Psychoanalysis and patristic and medieval theology proved more reliable companions in this quest than the optimistic rhetoric of liberal feminism. So, it has been a sustained struggle against many inhibitions and doubts to draw on my maternal experience in writing this, and I am still not sure I should be doing it.

My maternal life has continued to unfold in the ten years between writing that seminar paper and revising it today. I have become a grandmother five times over and have witnessed my daughter giving birth to my granddaughter. My mother died in 2016, leaving me with a sodden ache of loss and regret, love and guilt. I am glad that I was with her as she took her last struggling breath, as she was with me when I took my first struggling breath (Figures 1 and 2).

All this presses upon me as I ask what new insights I might offer and what challenges I might pose to theological writings about motherhood and birth, based on imaginative recollections and creative reconstructions of the ongoing phenomenon of my own maternal becoming.

But experience alone was not enough for the task I set myself when I first embarked on writing about what it means to mother. I needed academic resources – theologies, theories, and philosophies – to give shape to my reflections and filter my recollections through the intellectual mesh of argument and analysis, footnotes and citations. That was a new challenge.

Figure 1 With my mother – 1955

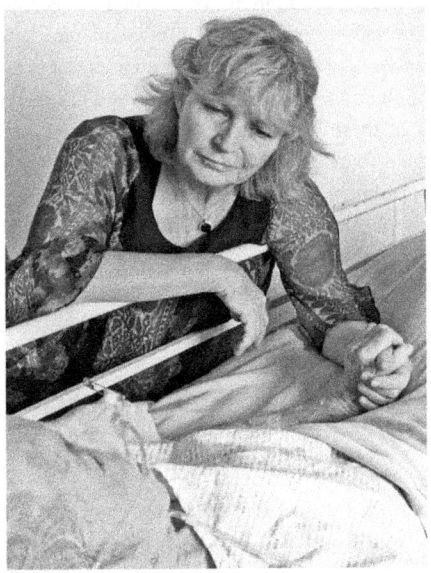

Figure 2 With my mother – 2016

1.2 Speaking of the Unspeakable

Having decided to offer a full-frontal exposure of my maternal body to academic scrutiny, I found myself floundering. Where were the linguistic and cultural lenses through which these experiences might be interpreted and rendered meaningful? Where were the theological and philosophical resources that offered a language adequate to the task?

I was familiar with the work of Kristeva and Irigaray, as well as some theorists whom they have influenced. Still, these were meagre pickings in the face of a vast philosophical and theological edifice produced by male thinkers perplexed and troubled by the fact of their own births. Often, these are focused more on the inevitability of death than on the gift of life, as in Heidegger's 'being toward death' or in Sartre's bookending of existential freedom and responsibility by the philosophically impossible absurdities of birth and death.

In her Hegelian-Marxist quest for a philosophy of birth, Mary O'Brien writes that the childbearing function has been regarded as natural and inevitable and therefore exempt from historical and philosophical analysis. It is either seen as a timeless truth of female existence that removes women from the sphere of politics and public life and assigns them to a domesticated maternal role to which they are naturally suited (for Hegel, vegetatively suited), or it is seen as a trap from which women must be liberated to achieve equal participation with men in social life. O'Brien writes that:

> Death has haunted the male philosophical imagination since Man the Thinker first glimmered into action, and in our own time has become the stark reality which preoccupies existentialism, an untidy and passionately pessimistic body of thought in which lonely and heroic man attempts to defy the absurdity of the void which houses his consciousness and his world. The inevitability and necessity of these biological events has quite clearly not exempted them from historical force and theoretical significance. We have no comparable philosophies of birth. (2007)

Lacking adequate resources with which to filter my voice through a distancing interpretative lens, I have plunged deeply into my memories of experiencing childbirth four times, weaving them into theoretical and theological reflections in the hope of discerning what might be described as a theology of maternity. (The spellchecker suggests changing that to 'materiality', which, for once, is not a ridiculous suggestion.) Influenced by the literary styles of Cixous, Irigaray, and Kristeva, I seek a voice that is affective and organic, a mimesis of the process by which maternal consciousness evolves through succeeding experiences of pregnancy, childbirth, and neonatal life, when the latter refers not only to the child but also to the mother.

This process of transitioning to motherhood now has a name – 'matrescence'. That word was initially used by American medical anthropologist Dana Raphael in an essay titled 'Matrescence, Becoming a Mother, A "New/Old Rite of Passage"' (1975). It refers to the need to recognise that adapting to maternal life is a rite of passage comparable to adolescence in the physical, psychological, and social upheavals it entails. In her book titled *Matrescence*, Lucy Jones writes, 'Everyone knows adolescents are uncomfortable and awkward because they are going through extreme mental and bodily changes, but, when they have a baby, women are expected to transition with ease – to breeze into a completely new self, a new role, at one of the most perilous and sensitive times in the life course' (2023: 13).

Of course, no written account can lay claim to an experiential immediacy that has not been reflected upon and interpreted, but the quest to weave a narrative around that primal shock of becoming a mother means struggling to find language equal to the task. As O'Brien points out: 'We cannot analyse reproduction from the standpoint of any existing theory. . . . There is no philosophy of birth, and yet it is of birth that we must theorize' (2007).

Writing of different stages of the I-Thou encounter, Martin Buber situates the relationship with nature at the most primal and wordless level: 'There the relation sways in gloom, beneath the level of speech. Creatures live and move over against us, but cannot come to us, and when we address them as *Thou*, our words cling to the threshold of speech' (1958: 6). This is also, according to Buber, the condition of the child in the womb, resting in a state of pre-personal life that is both natural and cosmic in its relationality (25–26). I imagine the embryo swaying in the watery darkness of the uterine sac to the rhythms of the maternal heart, the umbilical cord attached to the placenta, like a coral polyp swaying in the ocean, attached to the reef but dancing to the tides.

Yet if the unborn child constitutes the most natural condition of our species, what of the mother in whose body that mysterious creature is growing towards personhood? In what sense is she a person, and how might she articulate her relationship to that intimate and alien other? Feminist theorists argue that, lacking language to facilitate her transition from nature to culture, she becomes indistinguishable from what Buber describes as 'the womb of the great mother, the undivided primal world that precedes form' (25). The challenge that Irigaray poses is to bring this formless body into speech, to repair the ruptured relationship between words and the world. We need to

> find, rediscover, invent the words, the sentences that speak of the most ancient and most current relationship we know – the relationship to the mother's

body, to our body – ... We need to discover a language that is not a substitute for the experience of corps-à-corps as the paternal language seeks to be, but which accompanies that bodily experience, clothing it in words that do not erase the body but speak the body. (Irigaray, 1993a: 18–19)

Let me fast-forward to the improbable position I now occupy beyond the wildest imaginings of my younger self. My journey from a fifteen-year-old Presbyterian typist in Zambia to a radically left-leaning feminist Professor of Catholic Studies at the University of Roehampton in London is material for a different book. Suffice it to say that, if the birthing stories in this text rely on the creative recollections of my younger self, its academic content is more recent. Might there be resources available to me now, to which I had no access then, to ask what a theology of birth might look like if I drag that young mother into the language of academic research?

1.3 Methodicide

In the Book of Ruth, Boaz tells Ruth to glean in his field, to gather what the men have left: '"Stay here with the women who work for me. Watch the field where the men are harvesting, and follow along after the women." ... So Ruth gleaned in the field until evening' (Ruth 2: 8–9, 17). Perhaps it is the divinely appointed task of women theologians to follow in one another's footsteps, gleaning what is left in the margins when the men have had their fill.

Mary Daly calls upon feminist scholars to 'commit the crime of Methodicide, since the Methodolatry of patriarchal disciplines kills creative thought' (1990: 23). This is sound advice for my quest to discern the contours of a maternal theology by gathering gleanings from the margins of many more methodologically disciplined ways of harvesting knowledge.

I have already referred to my ambivalence about feminist theological methods based on the appeal to women's experience, but all my reflections here share the same loose association with established methods. In seeking creative freedom from more systematic or rationalised approaches, I have attempted to create the illusion of a 'natural' theological emergence, which reflects my personal and academic development over the time span covered here. This theological trajectory represents a struggle to allow the profound mystery of human becoming to be occasionally lit from within by a glimpse of otherness, an intuition of a presence beyond all that can be articulated or explained, yet which demands to be communicated. God is self-revealing, but such revealing only emphasises the utter hiddenness of the mystery behind the screens of language and conceptualisation. Like Mary, we can conceive of God in the depths of our being and ponder on these things in our hearts, but to breach this engulfing silence with descriptions and rationalisations feels like violation. At least, that is how it is for me.

If I am a theologian at all, I am one who has many more questions than answers, many more doubts than certainties, and never more so than when I seek to bring the complexities/complexes of mothering into theological focus. With Karl Rahner, I want to say that:

> It is the bitter grief of theology and its blessed task too, always to have to seek (because it does not clearly have present to it at the time) what, in a sense – in its historical memory it has always known. The history of theology is by no means just the history of the progress of doctrine, but also a history of forgetting. . . . What was once given in history and is ever made present anew does not primarily form a set of premises from which we can draw conclusions which have never been thought before. It is the object, which while it is always retained, must ever be acquired anew. (Rahner, 1974: 151–52)

The theological unfolding in this Element affirms Rahner's insight that, if we have 'the courage to ask questions, to be dissatisfied, to think with the mind and heart one actually has, and not with the mind and heart one is supposed to have . . . something will perhaps emerge which we ought to be thinking today' (153–4).

My academic research has always followed the promptings of my mind and heart because I came to academic theology too late in life and, as a relatively new Catholic following a pick 'n mix modular degree system in a secular university, I was not groomed in the proper ways of reading and interpreting theological texts. The taboos surrounding Mary in my brief flirtation with evangelicalism when my children were small had aroused an intense desire to better understand this maternal tradition – a desire that was laden with longings too deep for words. That is why my published monographs are weird ramblings through subterranean themes long buried by the modernising rationalisations of Catholic theology. My PhD explorations of Marian theology in dialogue with Irigaray led me to ante-Nicene writings (Beattie, 2002), where the history of theology did indeed yield rich fruits, not as new ways of thinking, but as historical gifts that could be 'acquired anew' in the quest for a maternal theology appropriate to our times.

In thinking with the mind and heart, my theology emerges not as an attempt to muster fluid, organic, and changing ideas about life's mysteries into a systematic account of how God might be discovered through mothering, but as a theology that follows the gestation and birthing process. I engage in a playful mimesis of maternal feminine language in the quest to break open sclerotic theological systems and open fertile incarnate possibilities. Just as my own faith and theological education have developed gradually over the time span I cover here, so my theological voice becomes more developed and recognisable as the writing unfolds.

References to phenomenology must similarly be treated with caution. While I acknowledge Mumford's influence in directing me towards the relevance of phenomenology for a maternal theology, I have been highly selective in my use of phenomenological insights. Most relevant to my purposes here is the quest to overcome the dualism that has divided post-Enlightenment Western thought, with its Cartesian and Kantian foundations, by affirming the materiality of consciousness in its dependence on bodily senses and perceptions. The body is neither a self-enclosed entity nor an addendum to consciousness. It is the tactile, visual, porous presence that incorporates us into the material world. Phenomenology invites us to discover anew the primordial existential reality through which the time and space of individual existence can be reintegrated into a wondrous and harmonious movement of dynamic encounters and relationships among and between material beings. This means that the appeal to experience is a necessary but not a sufficient condition for a phenomenological epistemology.

If there is a discernible method to what follows, perhaps it is best read not as a failed attempt at theology or phenomenology, but as the shaping of an unfinished narrative that is part memoir, part creative writing, and part theological reflection, leaving many questions unanswered. How could it be otherwise, when the quest leads us to the birthing (of) God? There should always be a little madness in our method when we risk speaking of the unspeakable.

There is, however, an important caveat. Modern popes distinguish between the (masculine) Petrine Church of institutions and hierarchies, and the (feminine) Marian Church of faith and devotion, insisting that the Marian Church is more important than the Petrine. I have written extensively on how this is a not-so-subtle and highly patronising attempt to justify the continued exclusion of women from the sacramental priesthood, but I am not advocating the dissolution of properly instituted and ethically accountable systems of authority and good governance into a charismatic ecstasy of maternal *jouissance*. Kristeva's psycholinguistic project warns that the overwhelming of the symbolic by the imaginary risks psychosis, through the unleashing of the unruly desires of the subconscious into an unregulated and anarchic psychological and social free-for-all. Indeed, in this era of populist politics and insatiable desires fuelled by capitalist consumerism, we might wonder if there is indeed a psychotic pandemic spreading through the Western democracies.

In appealing for a more fluid and incarnate symbolics shaped by the incorporation of birth and bodiliness into theological language, I am not suggesting it is either possible or desirable to return to a pre-oedipal state free from the necessary separation and socialisation of the earliest relationship between mother and child. I am arguing for more porous linguistic boundaries between reason and desire, body and soul, humanity and animality. My method is as much pre-modern as postmodern, harking back to the patristic and early medieval eras, before the rise of the universities (see Beattie, 2013, Chapter 8), when theology and spirituality, scripture and storytelling, nature and grace, cross-fertilised one another. This is a quest for a language capable of expressing what it means to be a bodily creature with animal needs and instincts, yet with a near-boundless capacity for delight and despair, conjured up out of unreliable memories and unrealisable dreams.

The emerging ethos of synodality introduced to the Catholic Church by Pope Francis may yet prove capable of accommodating the renewal of this fertile and creative synthesis, but that will require the overcoming of the primal fear of the female body that distorts and corrupts the doctrinal endeavour. Only the full incorporation of the female body into the graced sacramentality of the life of faith, including the sacramental priesthood, will allow for the development of an incarnational theology capable of providing a credible response to the challenges of our times. I am moving towards that conclusion in what follows.

PART II: CONCEPTIONS

2 Body

> Blindsided and increasingly isolated, I fell down a rabbit hole. I had gone, but I didn't know where, or if I would return. I found I was confronted with my selves anew: my childhood self, the bare, naked roots of early psychic disturbances. This, I did not expect. I thought early motherhood would be gentle, beatific, pacific, tranquil: bathed in a soft light. But actually it was hardcore, edgy, gnarly. It wasn't pale pink; it was brown of shit and red of blood. And it was the most political experience of my life, rife with conflict, domination, drama, struggle and power.
>
> (Jones, 2023: 10)

> To the world, I have selectively put forward those images of myself that conform to the trope of perfect motherhood. But it is among other mums, who are also bewildered, that the façade slips and I feel able to exhale and tell the truth. There, in that safety, I find that many of us are wrestling with this sense of maternal inadequacy.
>
> But what is this standard against which we all feel we are failing? Where does it come from, and why does it feel so pervasive?
>
> (McDonald, 2025: 6)

Nairobi, Kenya. It is late at night on 22nd August 1978. My baby was due to be born on 4th August, so I am having an induced birth. After labouring all day,

I have been wheeled into a delivery room in Nairobi hospital. Delivery. A word that suggests passivity and rescue, the mother being delivered of her child by medical experts.

Jomo Kenyatta, the first President of Kenya, died today, and my elderly white ex-colonial (not to be confused with postcolonial) doctor is in a flurry of agitation about what will happen to people like her. (Forty-seven years later, white Kenyans still live in comfortable affluence in one of the most beautiful countries on earth.) She frets and says that her hands are shaking. Through a fog of pain, I hear her say something about the baby being stuck. She asks for scissors, then complains that they are blunt. I will feel those blunt scissors every time I have sex for years to come.

I writhe, trapped in this no-man's land of childbirth, where raw animality triumphs over the conscious, cultured self.

The midwife at the natural childbirth classes told us that we would experience discomfort, not pain, when our babies were being born. She suggested we sing a song, keeping time by tapping our bellies during contractions. At some point during those unending hours, I abandon the song and the tummy-tapping when my taut belly begins to feel like a vast raw surface of exposed nerve endings, excruciating to touch.

Waves of pain rise up, lay claim to my exhausted body, drag me down, down, down. As they gradually relinquish their grip, I long to escape. I have never known such exhaustion, such impotence, such entrapment in the irresistible forces of nature that rise, rise, rise again beyond the threshold of the bearable and gnaw on me in jaws of steel.

As midnight approaches, some primaeval force heaves me over the endless struggle into darkness, pushing, grunting, sweating, shitting. The irresistible urge to push drives me forward through barriers of pain and resistance, squeezing my child's body into the world through my flesh and blood and bone. Then – a mighty all-consuming howling heave and the whooshing rush of birth. My baby slithers from my body in a torrent of blood that spurts all over the doctor, the floor, the birthing bed.

My first child is born. It's a boy. This is before the days of antenatal scans. We did not know what sex the baby would be.

I hear his cries and welcome his wrinkled, bloodied body into my arms. His face is crumpled and twisted with the effort of being born. The flurry of an emergency unfolds around me as the doctor begins to panic. Am I bleeding to death? I only know that I have given birth. I am ecstasy without end. Mine is the joy of 'deep, deep eternity' (Nietzsche). My husband, Dave, is crying.

I have had a postpartum haemorrhage. They consider a blood transfusion but decide to give me liver injections instead. Soon, when the AIDS pandemic oozes through the human bloodstream with its possible origins in Africa, I shall be glad of that decision.

Later, wide awake in my hospital bed, I am filled with unquenchable delight. Today, I might call it 'amazing grace', but my agnostic younger self would not have used such language. I want to maintain the indispensable myth that I am being true to my own story here.

A baby is crying in the nursery. It's my baby. I don't know how I know, but I know. My breasts know too. There's an unfamiliar contraction and tingling in my nipples as colostrum leaks through my hospital gown. Like the meconium that my baby will shit for the first few days of life, this is an unexpected substance – a miracle, perfectly balanced to introduce my little boy to the processes of human survival. Birth. Food. Defecation. Sex. Birth. Death. If you're lucky, they happen in that order. If you're not, life is birth, defecation, and death. I tell the nurse I want my baby. Tutting her disapproval, she brings his cot to my bed. I have just squandered my last good night's sleep for many years.

Dave arrives early the next morning, wan-faced and anxious. He spent what was left of the night lying awake, dreading the call from the hospital to tell him that the baby and I had died. So much blood. So much pain. But here we are. We've lived to tell the story, but what is this story?

2.1 Through a Mirror – Darkly

Years after that first birth, when my father died, I claimed the only inheritance worth claiming: his poetry. The poems that he wrote himself, and the battered old books that witness to his escape into other worlds, because this world never quite fulfilled its promises, never fully compensated him for the struggle of being born into it. Eventually, he smoked and drank himself out of it prematurely.

I found a poem by Alice Meynell, called 'Maternity', in one of those well-thumbed books:

> One wept whose only child was dead
> New-born ten years ago.
> 'Weep not; he is in bliss,' they said.
> She answered, 'even so,
>
> Ten years ago was born in pain
> A child not now forlorn.
> But oh, ten years ago, in vain
> A mother, a mother was born.'

In my seventieth year, I peer back through the mists of time to reconnect with that young woman being born as a mother as she gave birth to her first child at the age of twenty-three, not yet aware of the enormity of what lay ahead. I was naïve, less educated and more conservative in my opinions than I am now.

I was born and grew up in Lusaka, Zambia, and by the time I finished secondary school in 1970, there was no local provision of education beyond O Levels. Continuing to A Levels and university would have meant going to boarding school. Lying in bed at night, I used to listen to my parents discussing the options. My mother was conflicted. She told my father that she didn't want me to end up being a bookkeeper like her. She wanted better for me. But she also told people she was glad they had three daughters, not sons, because if they'd had sons, they would have had to leave Zambia for their education.

In the end, she suppressed her vicarious ambition for me to do better, and I did not want to go to boarding school anyway. We agreed that I would do typing classes at night school while working as an assistant in a jewellery shop during the day, a decision that she endorsed: 'Learn to type before you get married, Tina. Then if he ever leaves you, you'll be able to support yourself and your children'. (This year is our fiftieth wedding anniversary. He did not leave me.)

So there I was, former typist and newborn mother, exhausted and ecstatic, lying in a Nairobi maternity ward with my newone in a cot beside my bed. How could I have known in that mythologised bliss that this was the beginning of a lifelong journey of love and sorrow, adoration and rage, pride and shame, that would carve furrows in my soul and lay bare the deepest and most extreme passions that lurked within me, awaiting a catalyst powerful enough to ignite them? That catalyst was motherhood.

> A hunger remains, in place of the heart. A spasm that spreads, runs through the blood vessels to the tips of the breasts, to the tips of the fingers. It throbs, pierces the void, erases it, and gradually settles in. My heart: a tremendous pounding wound. A thirst. (Kristeva, 1987: 249)

2.2 Matrescence

My life is no longer my own. Milky nights and bleached days blur beneath a soggy blanket of love and loss. Heavy, aching breasts and the bloody ooze of afterbirth lay claim to my body. My clothes are permanently stained with milk, my shoulders cheesy and mildewed with baby vomit. Cramps and pains spiral through me as my uterus fists itself into something resembling normality, though it will never be the same again. My body is a stranger to me, my life an alien landscape mapped by my baby's incessant needs.

These uterine cramps are similar to the mild contractions that a pregnant woman feels before the onset of labour. These are known as Braxton Hicks contractions, named after the nineteenth-century English doctor who discovered them. He discovered them in the way that David Livingstone discovered Victoria Falls, though the indigenous people had always known they were there. They call them *Mosi oa Tunya* – the smoke that thunders. I am thunder and smoke, confusion and exhaustion, ecstasy and anguish, falling, falling, falling through mighty mists and torrents into the gorge of maternal life.

I wonder what we, the indigenous inhabitants, would call the female body if we were to lay claim to the right to name. What, for instance, might we call those pimples around our nipples which become more noticeable in pregnancy? They are called 'Glands of Montgomery' or 'Montgomery tubercles' because they were first described by Dr William Fetherstone Montgomery in 1837. What was the name of Caesar's mother, whose belly was sliced open in a procedure that bears the name of the son who was untimely ripped from his mother's womb?

If men are going to name our body parts, we might wish they were poets rather than scientists. John Donne did it so much more eloquently when he addressed his mistress going to bed:

> O my America! My new-found-land,
> My kingdom, safeliest when with one man mann'd,
> My Mine of precious stones, My Empirie,
> How blest am I in this discovering thee!

The imagery might be more seductive, but the conquest of the female flesh remains the same. Our bodies are mapped and named by the men who explore them, colonised by the linguistic empires of others, rinsed clean of meconium and colostrum and blood and slime and all that 'stuff', splinters of bone and fragments of flesh that cling to the underside of language, threatening to drag it down into silence and madness, into the womb/tomb of the other of being.

Phyllis Trible traces this phenomenon of ownership through naming back to the story of Genesis (Trible, 1978). When God brings the animals to the earthling, *'ādām*, the not-yet sexed human creature calls them by their names, asserting mastery over them. On first seeing the woman, the nuanced gendering of the Hebrew text makes him more clearly a man. (How would a man know what he was, unless there was another who was not like him?) He gives a cry of recognition but does not name her until after the fruit has been eaten, after the loss of innocence, after the fall. That is when he lays claim to her through the power to name.

> To the woman, he said,
> 'I will make your pains in childbearing very severe;
>   with painful labour you will give birth to children.
> Your desire will be for your husband,
>   and he will rule over you.' (Genesis 3:16)

Adam named his wife Eve, because she would become the mother of all the living. (Genesis 3:20).

Trible writes that: 'Now, in effect, the man reduces the woman to the status of an animal by calling her a name. ... Ironically, he names her *Eve*, a Hebrew word that resembles in sound the word *life*, even as he robs her of life in its created fullness' (Trible, 1978: 133).

The power to name. Braxton Hicks contractions. Montgomery's tubercles. Eve. Back in 1978, I could not have named that thick little spot on the vaginal wall that is connected to the clitoris, and which, according to the men of science, may or may not exist. That was only named in 1982 – the 'G-spot', after German gynaecologist Ernst Gräfenberg.

But men have yet to name some phenomena that are even more elusive than the G-spot. Perhaps they have no name. Long after the birth of my children, I'll discover the word *'jouissance'* when I start reading Lacan. Undaunted by the challenge of naming that which has no name, he writes: 'There is a *jouissance* proper to her, to this "her" which does not exist and which signifies nothing. There is a *jouissance* proper to her and of which she herself may know nothing, except that she experiences it – that much she does know' (Lacan, 1983: 144).

I know nothing, but this much I know. My newborn baby creates a turbulence in my soul beyond the power of words, beyond the control or consolation of any man. *Jouissance*, perhaps? 'In sensual rapture I am distraught. Nothing reassures, for only the law sets anything down. Who calls such a suffering jouissance? It is the pleasure of the damned' (Kristeva, 1987: 250).

Birthing has carried me along on a current too strong to resist. There is the terror that he will die, this child of mine. I am in the grip of a ferocious maternal urge to protect him, and a no less ferocious urge to get back the life that he has taken from me. I seethe with resentment that Dave still goes to work, comes home, has some existential world that has not been shattered and remade in the image of our child. I am undone. I am smoke and thunder and swirling rapids of love and dread. It will be many years before I find feminist theorists articulate and honest enough to analyse what I am experiencing: 'For many women, mothering begins in a fiercely passionate love that is not destroyed by the ambivalence and anger it includes' (Ruddick, 1990: 29).

I sensed then what science now confirms – that the changes brought about by childbearing reach deep into a woman's body and soul, so that she will never be the same again. Recent research suggests that changes during pregnancy and early mothering help adapt the brain to be finely tuned to the infant's needs. Lucy Jones refers to a research project led by neuroscientists Elseline Hoekzema and Erika Barba-Müller, which shows that changes associated with childbearing 'alter the neural basis of the self'. She quotes a conversation with Hoekzema, who explains that 'the observed brain changes are linked to all kinds of perinatal processes in the female body and behaviour, for example their physiological responses to infant cues, their nesting behaviour and their bonding with their infant in the postpartum period' (Jones, 2023: 118).

When I wrote the paper on which this Element is based, I quoted Wendy Wright to describe the existential transformation that motherhood brings about in a woman's life:

> One is never the same. After each birth, the body readjusts. But things are never as they were before. Silver-webbed stretchmarks are only an outward sign. More hidden are the now elastic vessels of the vascular system, the pliancy of muscle walls, the flat pouch of the once inhabited womb. Each child impresses upon waxen flesh the unique imprint of its life. Inscribes one's own life with an image all its own.
>
> Often I have thought how true that is of the heart as well. Each child occupies its own space and in growing presses and pushes out the bounded contours of one's heart. Each fashions a singular, ample habitation like no other. A habitation crowded with an unrepeatable lifetime of sorrow and joy. A habitation inscribed with a name. How could it be otherwise in the heart of God? (2002: 119)

Rereading that now, I wonder if the last question risks idealisation. Some feminist theologians suggest that a maternal God would be an antidote to the violence and tyranny of the God of patriarchal power and domination. Are they inadvertently colluding in the sentimental misrepresentation of maternal love, silencing and repressing the visceral, and sometimes violent realities of maternal experience? A mother's heart is a cauldron of conflicting and contradictory passions. If the heart of God experiences matrescence, then God is capable of the wildest excesses of passion and pain, love and fury, that the Bible attributes to its sometimes capricious and moody deity.

Lytta Basset's illuminating analysis of anger in the Bible, *Holy Anger: Jacob, Job, Jesus* (2007), invites the reader to see that anger can unleash transformative energy in the confrontation between self and the human or divine other. Basset offers an expansive theology of a biblical God who can be trusted with our most negative and furious emotions, redeeming them into life-giving opportunities for growth and deepened relationships.

In my earliest experiences of mothering, I had a faint recollection of the Presbyterian God of my childhood. Neither a tyrant nor a sacramentally incarnate mystery, God was both the gentle Jesus meek and mild of my evening prayers, and an intellectual proposition who, for a while, seduced my adolescent curiosity until sex proved more seductive. Maybe I would have welcomed Bassett's all-embracing, all-redeeming God of love and rage during the turbulence of matrescence, if I had encountered such a God. As it was, I remember neither prayer nor gratitude in response to the dark gift of my first child. I was love incarnate, and I was discovering the bloody, wounded realities of what that means.

2.3 Entering the Minefield

Struggling through the fog of matrescence in 1978, I lived in the dark shadow of the Good Mother. My child deserved a perfect mother, an endlessly patient, attentive adult who would respond to his every need in a spirit of total self-giving.

Peering back through time to those early years of mothering, I revisit Adrienne Rich's influential book, *Of Woman Born*, first published in 1977, a year before I became a mother. I feel an answering echo when I read these words:

> Every journey into the past is complicated by delusions, false memories, false naming of real events. But for a long time, I avoided this journey back into the years of pregnancy, childbearing, and the dependent lives of my children, because it meant going back into pain and anger that I would have preferred to think of as long since resolved and put away. I could not begin to think of writing a book on motherhood until I began to feel strong enough, and unambivalent enough in my love for my children, so that I could return to a ground which seemed to me the most painful, incomprehensible, and ambiguous I had ever travelled, a ground hedged by taboos, mined with false-namings. (Rich, 1977: 15)

Like Rich, Sarah Blaffer Hrdy uses the metaphor of the minefield to describe modern mothering. She writes, 'Today, mothers in developed countries, and with them fathers and children, enter uncharted terrain. . . . Bluntly put, motherhood has become a minefield, and we are walking through it without so much as a map to guide us' (2000: 5–6).

The new mothers in my circle of friends in the 1970s turned to books rather than older women and traditional practices. As daughters in the brave new world of liberal modernity, we would carve our own furrows through what none of us yet acknowledged was a minefield. Hugh Jolly's *Book of Child Care* (1975) was our go-to Bible, but others offered more radical and guilt-inducing guides to maternal perfection. Penelope Leach's *Baby and Child* (1977) insisted we direct our lives towards ensuring the child's happiness at all times. The mother was all in all, bonded and in bondage to the insatiable needs of her child. We read a book called *The Continuum Concept* (1975) by Jean Liedloff, who used her experience of 'Stone Age Indians' in the South American jungle to restore us to more natural ways of parenting children. Stone Age parenting is for Stone Age people, but how do we parent in between the ages, when we mistrust the old models and have yet to discover the new?

The nuclear family, playing out its dramas in privacy, lacks the communal bonds and networks of support that are part of child-rearing in more traditional cultures. Social media may be a mixed blessing, but the popularity of sites like Mumsnet attests to mothers' yearning to share their experiences and gain reassurance that they are not alone in their struggles. Looking back, I see how my generation tended to be more inhibited, obeying a taboo even among close friends that prohibited us from honestly sharing the sense of defeat, failure, and guilt that so often accompanied the shock of the newone. Books such as Jones's *Matrescence* and Chine McDonald's *Unmaking Mary* blow a cleansing wind of honesty through the fog of romanticism that surrounds the myth of the perfect mother.

Women of my generation have been groomed to denial and negation from birth, socially conditioned to model ourselves on impossible ideals of care, nurture, and self-sacrifice. As a result, years of struggling and failing to be the perfect mother can result in a burden of guilt and self-blame so cumbersome that maternal memories are blighted by shame. The haunting recollection of our episodic failures can overshadow what, for most of us, is, I suspect, a more benign and affirming reality involving attentive, conscientious, and joyful mothering.

I know from many conversations with other older mothers that the task of refiguring our maternal memories around the positive and life-giving aspects of our roles is a Sisyphean struggle against the nagging reminders of the times we failed to attain an unattainable ideal. As Sara Ruddick observes in her influential book, *Maternal Thinking*, 'Many mothers who live in the Good Mother's shadow, knowing that they have been angry and resentful and remembering episodes of violence and neglect, come to feel that their lives are riddled with shameful secrets that even the closest friends can't share' (1990: 31).

In her pioneering essay in feminist theology, 'The Human Situation: a Feminine View', published in 1960, Valerie Saiving reflects on what sin might look like from a feminised perspective. She suggests that the psychological conditioning of females into roles of passivity and submission might produce different temptations and sins from those that seduce the male psyche, conditioned to think in terms of active and competitive achievement and individuation. Writing of the demands of motherhood, Saiving observes that

> A mother who rejoices in her maternal role – and most mothers do most of the time – knows the profound experience of self-transcending love. But she knows, too, that it is not the whole meaning of life. For she learns not only that it is impossible to sustain a perpetual I-Thou relationship but that the attempt to do so can be deadly. The moments, hours, and days of self-giving must be balanced by moments, hours, and days of withdrawal into, and enrichment of, her individual selfhood if she is to remain a whole person. She learns, too, that a woman can give too much of herself, so that nothing remains of her own uniqueness; she can become merely an emptiness, almost a zero, without value to herself, to her fellow men, or, perhaps, even to God. (1960: 108)

Saiving's work is of its time and is not immune to criticism, but it remains a formative influence on the development of feminist theological reflection (Roundtable, 2012). Her caution about the impossibility of sustaining 'a perpetual I-Thou relationship' calls into question James Mumford's argument that maternal love calls for the total surrender of self to the needs of the helpless and vulnerable other.

In an insightful critique of Martin Buber's and Karl Barth's interpretations of I-Thou relationality, Mumford rightly points out that both presume some level of reciprocity and mutuality in the encounter, but this cannot be applied to the ethical responsibilities of mothering. He quotes Levinas: 'It may be conjectured that clothing those who are naked and nourishing those who go hungry is a more authentic way of finding access to the other than the rarefied ether of spiritual friendship' (Mumford, 2013: 49, quoting Levinas, 1989: 73). Neither Buber nor Barth provides an adequate ethical framework for reflection on the relationship between a mother and her unborn or newborn child, nor indeed – as Levinas points out – for any encounter between the strong and the vulnerable, the capable and the dependent, the clothed and the naked: 'The philosophy of dialogue ... idealizes encounters. One of the consequences of that idealization is to relegate the original encounter between newone and mother into the subpersonal realm' (Mumford, 2013: 77).

What goes unaddressed is the capacity of pregnancy, childbirth, and neonatal life to strip a modern mother of the psychological and physical resources by way of which she might respond to this unconditional, all-consuming demand for love. She stands isolated and alone, burdened with overwhelming responsibility for the life of the utterly helpless and dependent other who confronts her with insatiable need. As Saiving points out, this can be 'deadly' in its capacity to destroy a woman's sense of self and render her empty and worthless.

Good maternal practice is an acquired skill, not a natural womanly intuition. It entails channelling all those unruly and uncontrollable moods of matrescence into the disciplined task of learning to live as a dyad, neither consuming nor consumed by the voracious other who has carved out a space of co-existence with the coming into being of the maternal self. Ruddick argues that this entails a process of reasoning that cultivates the virtues necessary for that role, as in any other work, amidst the often-conflicting demands and desires of maternal life in societies distorted by patriarchal values. She writes, 'Actual mothers have the same kind of relation to maternal practices as scientists have to scientific practice, as believers have to religious practice. . . . [A]chievement, in maternal work, is defined by the aims of preserving, fostering, and shaping the growth of a child; insofar as one engages in maternal practice, one accepts these aims as one's own' (Ruddick, 2007).

In other words, motherhood requires an epistemology. That is a word I discovered in my first-year philosophy classes at university, several years after the birth of our fourth child. I thought they were saying 'episiotomy'. That word was in my lexicon. It was part of what I already knew, though I had no theory to explain it. The word had been carved into my flesh by blunt scissors, long before I conceptualised what it might mean.

There is a learning curve – an epistemological/episiotomical trajectory – that arcs away from that first birth into maternal life. This involves learning to balance one's individual needs, interests, and commitments with the responsibility to meet what Ruddick identifies as the three fundamental demands of the maternal role: 'These three demands – for *preservation, growth,* and *social acceptance* – constitute maternal work; to be a mother is to be committed to meeting these demands by works of preservative love, nurturance, and training' (1990: 17). In modern society, this is often a lonely process. We need to widen the lens to account for the many ways maternal life is shaped by social circumstances, genetic inheritance, and external influences beyond any individual woman's control.

2.4 Evolving Motherhood

The human emerges into the world not as a *tabula rasa*, but through a long evolutionary and relational story that imprints itself on every individual. We are born into states of radical dependency and extended relationships. Cultural and religious histories, socio-economic contexts, paternal and maternal genealogies, including predispositions to physical and mental illnesses and vulnerabilities, permeate and persist beyond each human life. Any attempt to shape a maternal ethics must begin not with the mother but with a web of relationships and influences.

Child psychoanalyst Erik Erikson emphasises the social dimension of childcare, arguing that healthy infant development is not the sole responsibility of the mother but requires a sustaining network of 'families to protect the mothers, societies to support the structure of families, and traditions to give a cultural continuity to systems of tending and caring' (1994: 116).

In *Mother Nature* (2000), Hrdy explores the evolutionary struggles, the conflicts and strategies of survival, perpetuated in our animal genes from generation to generation, as mothers and babies are locked in a mutual battle and embrace, tensed between birth and death, bonding and abandonment, survival or annihilation of the species. She refers to 'allomothering' to explain the scientific discovery that primates are communal in their parenting. The more dependent the newborn of the species, the more collective the endeavour to protect it and to raise it. In *Mothers and Others* (2009), she develops this theory to argue that the infant's dependence and the collaboration needed to ensure its survival have contributed to the evolution of our species. No wonder modern mothers go crazy in the isolation and bondage of those early months, closed up in the loneliness of the nuclear family home. They are, to use Hrdy's term, 'mired in maternity' (2000: 14).

Hrdy explains how the infant weaves its web of love around the mother, ensuring that she cannot escape. It rewards her dedication with feelings of pleasure and desire, so that the father becomes incorporated into the relationship through the seductive strategies of the newborn:

> Maternity is inextricably intertwined with sexual sensations, and it is an infant's business, through grunts and coos, touches and smells, to make the most of Mother Nature's reward system, which conditions a woman to make this infant a top priority. Evolutionary logic is firmly on the side of mothers who enjoy the sensual side of mothering for its own sake. (2000: 538)

The pleasure stimulated by the release of hormones during breastfeeding and by the infant's sensual nearness creates in the mother a deep sense of willing bondage in relation to the child's needs, and she, in turn, seduces the father into offering love and protection to the child. Those are the survival strategies that the newborn infant acquired in the ape-like infancy of our species. Our capacity to give what the infant needs to survive does not come naturally. It 'slumbers' within us, to use Hrdy's expression, and is awakened by a complex process of chemical arousal and emotional interaction in those early weeks.

Hrdy's analysis helps me to understand the strangeness of those early mothering months – the yielding of adoration and exhaustion to libido and seduction. The baby has a vested interest, a primal animal interest, in ensuring that the father stays around, born of its voracious need for bonding and love. Its survival can only be ensured by its ability to arouse and command love in those around it. Food and physical care might affect the formation of its body, but its earliest experiences of bonding or neglect will have a formative influence on its soul. All you need is love, so the song goes. The child attains its hold over the father by sexually arousing the mother and making her want him. The myth of Genesis expresses a profound truth about a woman's lot in life, with its warning of pain in childbearing and domination in marriage.

Becoming parents puts a strain on even the most stable and loving marriages, and we were no exception. Those intense and confusing emotions and bodily changes of early maternal life meant that I experienced our marriage as the best and the worst of worlds. I was grateful for the love and tenderness, the humour and companionship that our marriage provided, but I was resentful of Dave's freedom, his daily escape to work, the hobbies and interests he was still able to pursue. 'I just can't function as an individual anymore', I wailed, one particularly fraught evening when he walked in from his day at the office. That remains a joke between us when I feel put upon, but back then, it was no laughing matter.

All this, and mine was a privileged existence. In addition to a supportive husband and economic security, I had help with the house and the garden – I was living the expatriate lifestyle – but that only contributed to my boredom. There was nothing to do except look after the baby and drink endless cups of tea with other young mothers – all of us colluding in the myth that we were coping, all of us trying to outdo each other with the minuscule, tedious details of our babies' progress.

The privileges and comforts of middle-class life, however, are no antidote to the psychological stresses associated with matrescence. Jones observes that the new mothers she spoke to were experiencing struggles that were

> the result of twenty-first century parenting norms, which had become much more intensive, child-centred, and demanding than they ever had been before. These norms, combined with neoliberal economic policy, the erosion of community and the requirement for most families to have two incomes to live because of the ever-higher cost of living, were leading to staggering levels of tension, guilt and ill health among mothers. (2023: 13)

No wonder, then, that 'Suicide is the leading cause of death in women in the perinatal period between six weeks and one year after giving birth in the UK' (Jones, 2023: 14).

Jones describes the loneliness that festers beneath the mother and baby groups in which women seek company and consolation by putting a bright conversational gloss on their deepest, darkest feelings:

> At the mother and baby groups I attended, it seemed more and more as though we were all colluding not to say much at all, aware of the panopticon of surveillance, with society in the watch tower, waiting for us to slip up and

fail.... We new mothers didn't have the words to articulate the existential and emotional crisis of matrescence. I hadn't yet come across Rich's concept of the Institution of Motherhood. Without the words, I sank into a shameful, silent unhappiness. (2023: 147)

A rare, honest encounter with a mother who admitted that birth was 'fucking awful' was not enough to break the cover of silence. The two women shared dark laughter and enjoyed a welcome moment of solidarity and relief, 'But then we went back to the silence of our sealed-off, nuclear houses and submitted again to the myth of independence and self-sufficiency and individualism' (Jones, 2023: 149).

Despite the indolent indulgence of those neonatal months in Nairobi, I often felt close to the edge. How much greater the stresses must be for single mothers without any networks of support, for those struggling with poverty or homelessness, for victims of domestic abuse or violence, for those giving birth amid bombs and guns and shattered lives. There is a very long list of all that contributes to the distress afflicting many new mothers today, in the harsh, unforgiving glare of romantic social and religious demands for total, self-sacrificing servitude.

2.5 Moving Forward, Looking Back

My child and I survived that bloody night in Africa, when two of us were born. Just as he had to learn to be a fully human child, I had to learn to be a fully human mother. Those visceral instincts of birthing and bonding must yield to more reasoned practices of virtuous mothering. That is something I understand better now than I did then, when I did not anticipate the lifetime of learning that would stretch ahead of me as far as my own grave.

I had never heard of Adrienne Rich, Valerie Saiving, Sara Ruddick, or any of the other sources I draw upon in this journey back through birth and beyond. I was struggling to suppress feelings of intellectual frustration and inadequacy, knowing but unable to admit to myself or anybody else that I had given up on education and surrendered to domesticity far too soon. By the time my son was born in Nairobi, I had become immersed in the mind-numbing triviality of expatriate life. It would be another fourteen years before I finally registered as a mature student in Theology and Religious Studies at the University of Bristol, the year the youngest of our four children started school.

Let me go back now to the birth of that fourth child, another son. My first and last difficult experiences of childbirth frame two others that were closer to the serene ideal, to which I shall come later.

3 Blood

May 1985. We are living in Harare in Zimbabwe, with our three children. After the birth of our son in Nairobi, our daughter was born near Cardiff in South Wales in 1980, and our second son in Harare in 1983. In writing this, I am following the promptings of memory rather than chronology. In the order of time, two positive experiences of childbirth were a calm interlude between two that were chaotic and life-threatening. Those are the two that press upon me, demanding to be written first. So, back to 1985.

We briefly discuss having a fourth child. Dave reminds me that my longing to dedicate myself to writing and to develop a creative, intellectual dimension to my life alongside mothering will be deferred yet again. He asks if perhaps this is my intention – to be so distracted by the demands of motherhood that I don't have to face down my fear and insecurity to respond to that deep yearning that has been in me since childhood – to write. I insist I can do it all and have it all. Have babies, write books, be all I want to be. I stop taking the pill.

8th May 1985. My father dies of a heart attack. He is fifty-eight. He's always had a thing for numerical symmetries and coincidences, but surely dying at 58 on 8.5.85 is going too far? Emphysema and alcoholism have finally laid claim to his beloved body and his troubled, vulnerable, beautiful soul. He, too, was a writer who squandered his gifts on distractions. A lover of poetry and music, his youthful hopes withered in self-doubt and frustration.

He wrote a poem on New Year's Eve in 1954, anticipating the birth of his first child (Figures 3 and 4).

It was one of the sorrowful blessings of my life to be that child he anticipated with such youthful optimism, to watch as the hopes faded, the poetry fell silent, and his soul grew weary.

May 1985. He is dead. My world fades to grey. I cannot see colours. I am living, but I'm not alive. My little ones orbit around me at a vast distance. I tend to their needs, but something vital is missing. This is not the time to have another child. I go back on the pill.

Gradually, pastel shades of hope seep into the world. We take trips to game parks, bouncing and jostling over dirt tracks, pitching our tent in unfenced campsites where baboons bicker and snicker in the trees above us, and elephants trundle past to drink at the river's edge at sunset. Our little ones scramble in the dust and laugh at my warnings. I am anxious about snakes and scorpions, not to mention lions growling nearby through the African night. But we want our children to love the wilds of Africa as much as we do, so I quell my anxieties and enter into the spirit of their delight.

But another anxiety is churning inside me. It's as if my body is in mourning for my father. I'm bleeding at intermittent intervals. I'm exhausted. I'm putting on weight. Eventually, I go to the doctor.

'Mrs Beattie, how many children have you had?'
'Three.'
'And you didn't realise you're four months pregnant?' he says, incredulous.

Miraculously, when I should have been resting in bed to save the threatened pregnancy, the baby has hung on in there through it all, but the bleeding is a bad sign. I have to rest, avoid exertion, and even refrain from lifting my little boy, who, at two years old, still wants to be carried.

The pregnancy develops, and the bleeding worsens. I have a condition known as *placenta praevia*, in which the placenta covers the opening of the uterus. As

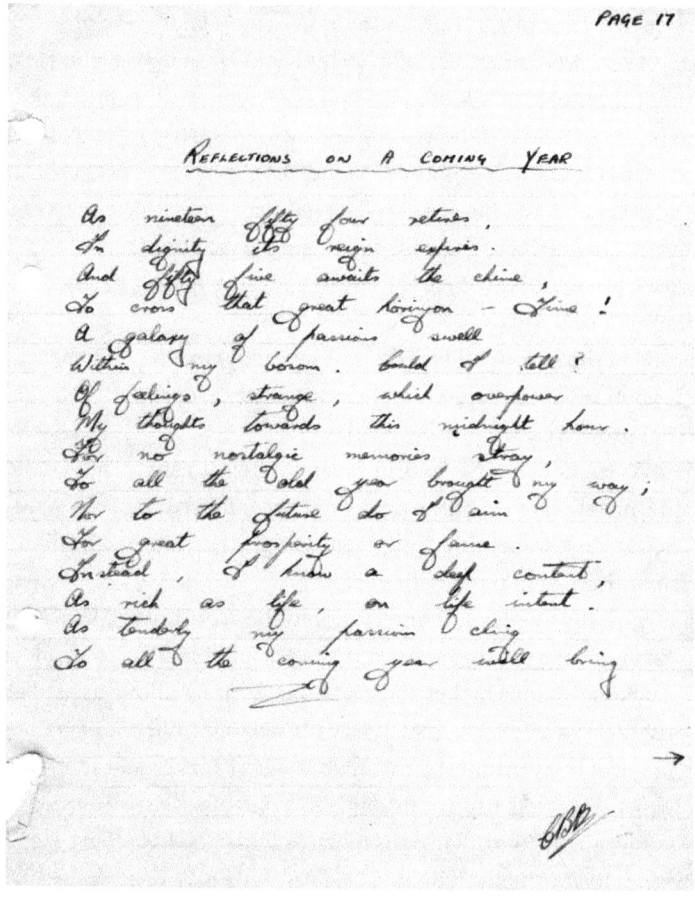

Figure 3 My father's poem – 1954

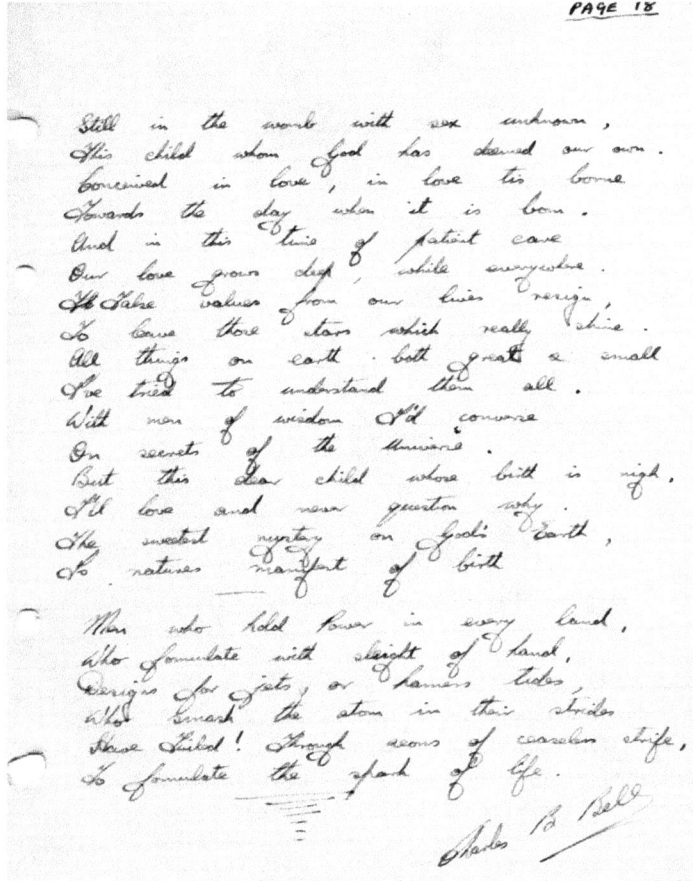

Figure 3 (cont.)

the baby grows, the placenta peels away from the wall of the uterus, severing the blood vessels delivering nourishment to the child. I become prone to sudden haemorrhages. Bloodied sheets and sodden clothes. Emergency trips to the hospital. A growing sense of dread about what this means for the child in my womb.

3.1 Decoding Blood

Blood is the most primal substance. Our ancient and medieval ancestors believed that body fluids such as semen and breast milk were different forms of blood. In medieval theology, art, and devotion, 'blood bubbles up everywhere' (Bynum, 2007: 9), signifying complex meanings associated with fertility and injury, delight and trauma, passion and cruelty. In her study of medieval blood symbolism, Bettina Bildhauer attributes

Figure 4 With my father – 1955

> the importance given to blood as basically granting access to the truth and as binding body and soul to each other while separating them from the external world. . . . Because blood is believed to hold body and soul together, it is often blood contained inside the body that is valued positively, while it is a sign of danger if blood has escaped. (Bildhauer, 2013)

What then are we to make of the birthing body, in which water and blood are shed in the parting of body from body, delivering mother and child into the newness of life or the darkness of death?

The bleeding female body disrupts the sacrificial shedding of blood that constitutes men's religious rituals. It is much easier to interpret male blood, which is always a sign of injury or disease, than it is to decode the many meanings associated with female blood. Every woman has a complex relationship with her blood from puberty to the menarche. She must read the signs and interpret the meanings (see Beattie, 2006: 348–355).

So let's talk about blood and death, and why, when a pregnant woman looks in the mirror, her reflection may be a *memento mori*.

My first pregnancy had already given me new insights into the potent significance of blood, beyond the menstrual rhythms that had patterned my body and moods since puberty. Six weeks into that first pregnancy, smears of blood warned of a threatened miscarriage. My old-fashioned doctor recommended purdah for a few weeks, and the pregnancy continued. As the baby took root, the effects of his presence began to show in my swelling belly, my ripening breasts, the swollen purple flesh of my labia. Pregnancy is not a disease, and mine was a much-wanted pregnancy, but even so, these involuntary changes render one's familiar body strange and unsettling.

During that first pregnancy, my blood yielded up its secret. I had inherited the Rhesus Negative blood group from my father. If my child were Rhesus Positive, it would trigger antibodies that would attack any future Rhesus Positive child in my womb, so that each pregnancy would result in increasingly sick and disabled infants. Here is how the website of the National Health Service (NHS) describes it:

> Rhesus disease only happens when the mother has rhesus negative blood (RhD negative) and the baby in her womb has rhesus positive blood (RhD positive). The mother must have also been previously sensitised to RhD positive blood.
>
> Sensitisation happens when a woman with RhD negative blood is exposed to RhD positive blood, usually during a previous pregnancy with an RhD positive baby. The woman's body responds to the RhD positive blood by producing antibodies (infection-fighting molecules) that recognise the foreign blood cells and destroy them.
>
> If sensitisation occurs, the next time the woman is exposed to RhD positive blood, her body produces antibodies immediately. If she's pregnant with an RhD positive baby, the antibodies can cross the placenta, causing rhesus disease in the unborn baby. The antibodies can continue attacking the baby's red blood cells for a few months after birth. (NHS, 2025).

All my children are Rhesus Positive. This is natural childbirth. A mother's body sometimes wages war on her unborn child. It's all in the blood and the genes. Thank God that science has denatured childbirth.

3.2 A *Via Dolorosa*

I am about thirty-four weeks pregnant. It's hard to be precise under the circumstances. I'm in hospital after another haemorrhage, when blood begins gushing from my vagina and can't be stopped. I am rushed to the operating theatre for an emergency caesarean. The surgeon tells Dave that they are doing it to save the mother. They might not be able to save the baby. Such are the choices we sometimes face.

There is a tragic dimension to pregnancy and motherhood. To conceive is to set out upon a *via dolorosa*, no matter how much one longs for the child. The only inevitability after birth – and sometimes before birth – is death.

The feminist critique of patriarchy focuses primarily on repressed emotions of fear, revulsion, and violence associated with the potent capabilities and deadly associations of the maternal body. But fear is also a consequence of love and vulnerability, of the vulnerability that is love. There is the terror that the unborn child will kill its mother, the beloved, in the process of being born, and the guilt of those who caused their mothers to suffer and maybe to die by being born. 'We are doing this to save your wife. We might not save the child'. What if they save neither? What if they save the child and not the mother? Who must he then become, this man of mine and father to the three small children waiting at home as their mother bleeds, to birth, perchance to die?

Tolstoy tells it well in *Anna Karenina*, with its eloquent juxtapositions of birth and death. The peasant Levin recalls the death of his brother a year earlier, when he hears that his beloved wife Kitty is in labour:

> All he knew and felt was that what was happening was what had happened nearly a year before in the hotel of the country town at the deathbed of his brother Nikolay. But that had been grief—this was joy. Yet that grief and this joy were alike outside all the ordinary conditions of life; they were loopholes, as it were, in that ordinary life through which there came glimpses of something sublime. And in the contemplation of this sublime something the soul was exalted to inconceivable heights of which it had before had no conception, while reason lagged behind, unable to keep up with it. (Tolstoy, 2012)

Reason has always lagged behind, unable to keep up.

They save us both, though our baby is a tiny scrap of life, just over five pounds in weight. That's almost half the weight of our first child when he was born.

Is the baby alright? My closest friend has a six-year-old daughter, Lee, whose cerebral palsy is the result of a traumatic and mismanaged birth. I have seen what it takes to care for a profoundly disabled child, with an abundance of love and sorrow that I can scarcely imagine. Would I be capable of such unconditional, suffering love?

The caesarean leaves an indelible imprint on my body. Silver stretch marks have already left cryptic traces on my breasts and thighs, but now a scar pouts atop my pubic hair. It shouldn't matter, but it does. I resent this small but unsightly disfigurement.

The wound heals, but I cannot shake off a sense of apathy. Our baby boy is fretful, and I watch him anxiously for signs of birth damage. Breastfeeding is hard to establish. After a few months of painful struggling with cracked nipples, I develop an abscess. Dave finds me collapsed on the bathroom floor, feverish and fainting. I offer my children the rudiments of mothering, stripped of laughter and fun and lightness of being. Bereavement, blood loss, surgery and its aftermath, broken nights with a baby who seems as distressed by the conditions of his birth as I am, have left me feeling like a husk of myself, weighed down by a burden of guilt about the insufficiency of my ability to mother my children with all the abundance of patience and play that I desire for them – that society tells me I owe them.

3.3 Placental Mediations

The placenta is a miracle and a parasite, even when it grows and functions as it should. Hrdy cites research on the placenta that seeks to explain its voracious plundering of the maternal body. The father's genes activate its development, and its complex chemical mechanisms and nurturing functions ensure that his child thrives by commandeering the mother's bodily substance and her attention, even at the expense of her other children, who may not be his. The placenta has been described as 'a ruthless parasitic organ existing solely for the maintenance and protection of the fetus, perhaps too often to the disregard of the maternal organism' (Hrdy, 2000: 433). One research project describes the placenta as a 'battleground' and refers to 'the cryptic conflict in livebearing species during pregnancy':

> Specifically, while it is in the interest of both parties that the fetus is born, the mother also needs to provide for other offspring, both current and future. However, for each offspring (and its father) it is better if the mother devotes all her resources to that offspring. Thus, the conflict becomes an arms-race between mother and fetus over the allocation of her resources during gestation; in mammals the placenta is the battleground where this conflict is fought. (Queen's University Belfast, 2025)

An article in *The New York Times* uses the language of an invasive military force: 'Every minute, about 20 per cent of the mother's blood supply flows through the placenta. The front line of the invasion is a cell called a trophoblast, from the outer layer of the embryo. Early in pregnancy, these cells multiply explosively and stream out like a column of soldiers' (Grady, 2014).

An arms-race. A battleground. The front line. Explosions. A column of soldiers. Science is never free from cultural influences. Scientists choose their language, and that linguistic prism through which facts are refracted shapes the meanings we attribute to the phenomena we observe (Laqueur, 1990; Soskice, 1987). In late capitalism with its militarised powers and ruthless competitiveness, we survive or die by conquest or defeat. All is violence and violation, a struggle to the death, as Darwinism overflows the boundaries of established scientific hypothesis to become the explanatory narrative that shapes our economics, our politics, our sex lives, and now even our placental relationships.

This is a very different symbolics from the meanings and rituals associated with the placenta in some pre-modern religions and cultures, which are now being reclaimed by some modern practitioners (Campbell, 2019). The maternal body is a dynamic, mysterious locus of change and exchange, an evolutionary microcosm within which perhaps the whole human story unfolds again and again, from the watery cellular conceptus through to the fully developed infant. Medieval theologians and natural philosophers (scientists) believed that the child in the womb developed through all the different life forms – from vegetative to animal to human. That was why they regarded early abortion before quickening (foetal movement) as a lesser sin than late abortion.

The placenta is part of this wondrous process of human becoming. It has analgesic properties, which might explain why many mammals eat it shortly after giving birth. It soothes the pain and enables the mother to tend to her young (Hrdy, 2009: 216). For some theologians, it presents a metaphysical quandary worthy of academic speculation: 'On the basis of the application of several important metaphysical concepts to our biological observations of the placenta, we argue that there is sufficient evidence to support our claims regarding the metaphysical status of the placenta' (Gremmels et al., 2014: 333). Might we think of the Holy Spirit as a placenta, mediating between God the Father and God the Son, soothing the sorrow of love in a placental economy of divine subsistence?

3.4 Trinitarian Speculations

David Cunningham suggests such an analogy in his quest to articulate the trinitarian mystery. Here is what he writes:

> In a pregnancy, a woman must go forth from herself and become other to herself *twice*: first in conception, and again in the production of an organ of mediation between mother and child (the placenta). If we were to name the relations that thereby develop within pregnancy, we might call them 'motherhood' and 'childhood'; and the production of the placenta creates an additional relation of (let us say) 'mediating.' Note that these relations are not simply 'among' three separate entities; the mother, child and placenta are all interconnected and, at times, not even clearly distinguishable from one another. (2003: 82)

The more I reflect on this, the more puzzled I become. I confess I never found it difficult to distinguish myself from the placenta, even if the embryo made a more complex claim upon my identity. I don't think I seriously considered the placenta until it threatened my life.

Is the mother a biological organism on a par with the placenta and the zygote? Did I 'go forth' from myself when I conceived? Given that I was four months pregnant with our fourth child before I discovered the cause of my gynaecological troubles, I spent half of that eight-month pregnancy not even knowing of the baby's existence. If he had been washed away in one of those early bleeds, would I even have known?

Conception is the most hidden as well as the most momentous of events. A woman knows nothing about it. Even if it was a moment of sublime orgasmic delight, do we really go out of ourselves in such moments? Do we not instead come home to ourselves most fully when the soul's yearning for union experiences an epiphany of satisfaction before the chasm opens up, wider and deeper than before, because the beloved other is, after all, just the same old other, and the divine moment, the moment of divination, has passed? Mystics use the language of sex to describe union with God, because it is not a going forth but a homecoming, not a becoming other but a becoming nothing and everything in the presence of the other. No wonder they use such language interchangeably with being a child in the womb or an infant in the arms of its mother. To quote Michael Hahn and Lydia Shahan (2024): 'Mystical writers employed the language of pregnancy, childbirth and motherhood to describe an intimate relationship with a God who was both human and divine. In doing so, they sought connections between mystical relationality and one of the most intensely intimate human experiences of embodiment, in its joy and pain, intimacy and alienation, fulfilment and loss' (201).

There might well be a solitary successful sperm burrowing into an ovum in the post-coital unknowing of the woman's body. As Kristeva writes: 'Cells fuse, split, and proliferate; volumes grow, tissues stretch, and body fluids change rhythm, speeding up or slowing down. Within the body, growing as a graft, indomitable, there is an other. And no one is present, within that simultaneously dual and alien space to signify what is going on. "It happens, but I'm not there"' (Kristeva, 1980: 237).

Whatever the circumstances of conception, there might be an awesome pilgrimage of life going on inside a woman's body in which her desires and intentions count for little. St Augustine thought that a man's inability to control his erections with the power of his rational mind was a sure sign of original sin. What might we say about a woman's inability to control her body's reaction to ejaculation, as the moment of a man's orgasm becomes for her the beginning of a life-changing process, in which her own volition and pleasure have little role to play?

Our medieval forebears believed that a woman only conceived if she, too, had an orgasm, which was a mixed blessing. It might have made their husbands skilful in the art of love, but a woman who fell pregnant through rape was at risk of being accused of deriving unwarranted pleasure from the act, for how could she fall pregnant unless she had an orgasm? Modern science places no such demands on a man's skills of seduction and foreplay, and no such limits on the potential consequences of rape.

So what of that trinitarian metaphor which suggests that a woman 'goes forth from herself' when she conceives and when the placenta is produced? Neither of these is a conscious process over which she has any control. As Margaret Kamitsuka observes: 'Gestating a foetus demands extraordinary corporeal self-giving. The foetus and the placental organ will take what they need, irrespective of the pregnant person's desire to give less or not to give at all. Gestational hospitality happens before it is even offered' (2024b: 345).

3.5 Biological Conceiving and Maternal Becoming

I question Cunningham's suggestion that his trinitarian analogy, though imperfect, might provide an example unique in nature for the interconnected relationships of the Trinity. The biological process of conception does not constitute a woman's going forth from herself into pregnancy. She goes forth when she makes the transition, whether willingly or unwillingly, from being a woman who discovers she is pregnant to agreeing to become a mother. The 'going forth' is an act of desire and will, not an act of biology.

But how can a woman go forth in the production of a placenta? The biological process of placental formation enables the flow of life-giving fluids from the no-longer-self of the mother's body to the not-yet-other of the developing foetus, but the going forth of mother and child will be forged in the afterbirth, in the post-placental transition from animality to humanity. Motherhood and childhood are ways of being that we acquire through time, shaped by the cultural, historical, and domestic circumstances within which we give birth and are born. In that process, we become bound by the Kantian imperative that we must never treat another person only as a means to an end, for every person is an end in herself. However, the placenta is a means to an end, a temporary organ discarded once it has fulfilled its purpose.

It is difficult to see how this compares, even analogously, to the role of the Holy Spirit. Christians believe that the Holy Spirit is the Third Person of the Trinity, mediating the active love and wisdom of God in the co-eternal perichoresis of intra-trinitarian relationships. The placenta, on the other hand, has no personal attributes and no enduring significance. Its function ceases when the child is born, after which it is disposed of (or eaten), with or without a ritualised honouring of its temporary significance.

Perhaps, though, the analogy would work if we stretched the placental metaphor almost to breaking. Like the Holy Spirit, the placenta could become an elusive metaphor for the sensible transcendental – to borrow Irigaray's expression – as the medium within which self and other are incorporated into material exchanges of fertile, nurturing love that constitute a divinised space capable of accommodating difference without destruction or consumption. Like Kamitsuka, Irigaray uses the language of hospitality to express this, suggesting that the placenta provides a place within the mother 'that does not belong to the one or the other, but permits their coexistence' (Irigaray, 2013: 44). This might invite an analogy with the relationship of the Holy Spirit to the Father and the Son, but it may also suggest something of the nature of maternal love, which retains its visceral potency amid the complexities of the evolving mother/child relationship.

A good mother must learn to love and let go, to bond and to liberate, weaving an umbilical cord of attentive solicitude and unconditional love that winds from the placental riches of the maternal heart to the needs and desires of the growing child. Genuine relationships fall short of this ideal, but in the depths of her being, does any mother forget her child? When women have had abortions, they nearly always express sadness for the life they could not bring to fruition, even if they do not regret the decision. A woman whose children are taken into care suffers devastating loss. And there is perhaps no well of sorrow as deep and dark as the maternal heart when a child dies. No wonder that the closest analogy the prophet can find for the love of God is the love of a mother for her child:

> Can a mother forget the baby at her breast
> and have no compassion on the child she has borne?
> Though she may forget,
> I will not forget you!
>
> (Isaiah 49:15)

The placenta is obsolete once the child is born, but the mother will never break free of the umbilical flow that binds her forever to the life of her child. And yes, sometimes this becomes a battleground, a struggle for survival against the forces of death. The child must pull away to give birth to the 'I', and the maternal heart haemorrhages in abjection beyond all that can be said of love.

3.6 A Deadly Vocation?

Two births so far, though chronologically they were my first and my last, with two in between. Two near deaths. An estimated 800 women die every day in childbirth, most of them in sub-Saharan Africa, where three of my four children were born.

800 women. That is the equivalent of two jumbo jets crashing every day, but these are poor women. Some of them make their last journeys in wheelbarrows and donkey carts, jostling over rugged paths too late to seek the medical

attention they need. They matter less in the eyes of the world than those who can afford to travel in planes and, very occasionally, die as a result.

Pope Francis (2013) called for the Church's priests to be shepherds who had the smell of the sheep, but he, too, fell under the spell of the maternal romance. In his poor church of the poor, nearly 300,000 maternal deaths every year did not merit a mention. The Church that has the smell of the sheep has yet to acquire the stench of an infected womb resulting from a botched abortion.

To dichotomise female blood as a sign of nature, fecundity, and birth, and male blood as a sign of culture, sacrifice, and death, is to forget that, until the twentieth century, and still today for the world's poorest women, childbirth is as much about early death as new life. While statistics about maternal mortality include many variables depending on the quality of data, there is incontrovertible evidence that poor women and those living in regions of war and humanitarian crises are at significantly higher risk of dying from childbirth-related causes than those in more affluent areas with access to good obstetric care.

UNICEF (2025) reports a significant 40 per cent drop in maternal mortality rates during the first quarter of the twenty-first century, from an estimated 328 deaths per 100,000 live births in 2000 to an estimated 197 deaths per 100,000 live births in 2023. This is good news, but nearly 300,000 women still die every year from avoidable obstetric complications or unsafe abortions. In 2020, there were an estimated 1,223 maternal deaths per 100,000 live births in South Sudan (one of the world's most war-torn and violent regions), while in Norway and Poland, this falls to 2 in 100,000 women. This is as much about social and economic justice as it is about war and poverty. Nigeria is one of the wealthiest countries in the world, but with an estimated 1,047 deaths per 100,000 live births, it has one of the highest maternal mortality rates (CIA.gov, 2025). In both the United States and Britain, a black woman has a significantly higher risk of dying in childbirth than a white woman (Curry, 2023; Omotoso, 2024).

In their book, *Half the Sky* (2010), Nicholas D. Kristof and Sheryl WuDunn point out that the majority of maternal deaths occur in the third trimester, as a result of lack of access to emergency obstetric care. Here is Colleen Carpenter Cullinan's description of what happens to a woman when she has an obstructed labour, as I did, but with no medical attention – a process that can last for up to a week:

> The baby usually dies after the first few days, but is only born much later, when the mother's body has been so injured by the unrelenting pressure of the child's body pushing against hers – resulting in a good bit of her living skin and muscle and tissue dying from lack of blood flow – that her body rips apart and frees the dead child at long last. In the best case scenario, the tear opens her bladder and she is left incontinent, unable to contain a constant flow of

urine. In the worst case, the tear opens not only her bladder but her rectum, and both feces and urine spill forth from her body in a relentless, unstoppable flow that – without surgical repair – will last for the rest of her life. Some women also have nerve damage and find themselves unable to move their legs properly, or at all. So a child born dead, grievous untended internal injuries, filth, stench, perhaps even paralysis. Of course, this is only the beginning: who would live with such a creature? She smells, she cannot keep herself clean or dry, she is not fit for society and barely fit for work. Her husband leaves her. The other women of the village shun her. Her child is dead. (Cullinan, 2008: 1–2)

We might tweak Gregory of Nazianzus's words and apply them not to the prenatal newone but to the ravaged mother:

> a terrible, pitiable sight, unbelievable to anyone who did not know it was true: human beings both dead and alive, mutilated in most parts of her body, scarcely recognisable either for who she is or where she comes from. ... She has been made in the image of God in the same way you and I have. (Gregory of Nazianzus [modified], quoted in Mumford, 2013: 185)

God, too, is torn apart in childbirth – but I shall come to that later.

The close link between economic justice and childbearing leads me to question Mumford's rejection of the social contract as a resource for the ethics of birth. If we pare it down to the most utilitarian language, society depends on women's willingness to bear children. In return, women are entitled to material care and support, including health care and economic and social security. It is a truism that it takes a village to raise a child. In modern societies, the 'village' comprises the tax-funded institutions that hold the social fabric in place through the just allocation of resources.

But no social system, however just, can protect us from the existential realities, exigencies, and sometimes unbearable sorrows that constitute the human condition with its bookends of birth and death. Feminist theorists such as Irigaray risk inverting, but thereby reinforcing, the same old dualisms when they assert the primacy of birth over death, of fecundity over sacrifice. In the midst of birth, we are in death, and every birthing encompasses a dying. The only guarantee we can make to that newone into whom our life force has flowed, in whom our hopes and dreams, our terrors and vulnerabilities, are enfleshed, is that one day, this child too must die. To give birth is to make a blood sacrifice, a sacrifice of one's own blood. It is to say, 'This is my body, this is my blood, given for you'.

But not every birth is so closely associated with death. Sometimes, a birth is indeed a defiant affirmation of life that sends death running for cover to bide his time in the shadows of the passing years.

3.7 Changing Places

Soon after that last traumatic birth, and after many discussions and arguments, we packed up and moved to the savage country that was Thatcher's England. The grey postnatal months blurred. I found myself huddled in a small house in an alien culture with four little children, wondering if this was it. Was this all there was to life?

There were the usual mother-and-baby groups, but I had outgrown them. The walls closed in on me, and my brittle, bright façade hid a growing sense of despondency and isolation.

There was consolation in the enduring power of friendship, as perhaps there always is for women. By a minor miracle of grace, my closest friend, Ingrid, Lee's mother, had also moved from Zimbabwe to the UK with her husband and four children. Ingrid and I propped each other up emotionally during those difficult early years. After another long outpouring of my frustration and boredom, she suggested I should consider going to university.

Never had I imagined it would be possible to make up for those lost years of education. I applied to the University of Bristol as a mature student in the Department of Theology and Religious Studies, and practised saying 'Schillebeeckx' to impress them during the interview. I knew next-to-nothing about academic disciplines and degrees, but I opted for Theology and Religious Studies because all my most profound questions were God-shaped. The University offered me a place. In 1991, when that little boy whose early survival had seemed so precarious started school, I became an undergraduate student.

Lee died at the age of thirty-five on my 57th birthday – 16th March 2012. To her, I owe some of my deepest insights about the fragility and finitude of life, and its drenching in exquisite epiphanies of joy, freedom, and friendship amidst the sorrows. Lee lived to the fullness of her being – in shouts and cries of delight, in howls and torrents of anguish, in unquenchable nowness of being. Lee, too, is an unanswerable question about life and its meanings, its beginnings, and its endings.

4 Birth

6th May 1980. Upper Church Village, near Pontypridd, Wales. I am in labour. Our daughter may never entirely forgive us for her birth taking place in the least exotic place we've ever lived in.

This second pregnancy has been a time of relative contentment with my toddler and my swelling belly. I awake in the small hours, with the first cramps of labour. When my waters break, we ask our neighbour to come and look after our little boy, and we go to the hospital. They leave me sitting in a corridor, dribbling water down my legs, while they try to find my file. Eventually, it's located, and I'm allocated a bed in a twin room.

Behind the screens, the woman in the other bed is having a noisy time of it. She keeps shouting at her husband to wake up.

'Wake up! Wake up! I'm having another pain'.

A midwife arrives and asks the husband to leave while she examines his wife. As he leaves, he vents his exhaustion and frustration: 'I hope they chop your bloody legs off', he says, leaving me wondering how much he understands about the process of birth.

She is wheeled away to a delivery room. When I see her with her baby in the ward afterwards, there appears to be no significant harm to her legs. The nurse tells me that her husband fell asleep in his car and missed the whole thing.

My labour progresses smoothly, with a sense of calm assurance that this time, I am in control. But does any woman control that most animal of functions, when nature takes over in the birthing of a child?

The sun rises soft and benign over the Welsh hills, ushering in a warm, blue spring day – a good day for being born. As the waves of pain grow, I ride the crests and rest in the troughs, surfing my suffering. They push me to the delivery room. There are two midwives and my husband. When the contractions become intense, I cling to one of the midwives and beg her not to leave me, as I bury my face in her neck.

More than forty years later, I can still close my eyes and remember the smell of her perfume. Sometimes I wonder if my mother wore the same perfume when I clung to her, wanting more of her than any mother can give. The midwife is mothering me, and I am breathing in her scent.

Blue Grass. That was the name of the perfume my mother used to wear.

I never wore perfume while breastfeeding. I wanted to smell only of myself, attached to my baby by whatever pheromones our bodies were transmitting beneath the level of consciousness. Soon, that animal relationship would be overlaid by the subtle interventions of language, culture, and consciousness, but I savoured the savage sensuality of that newborn intimacy.

As labour progresses, I become confused. This is what they call the transition stage. I long to push, but the midwife tells me not to. She tells me to pant. The urge becomes irresistible. She checks again, poking around my cervix. Yes, it's fully dilated. All systems go.

The other midwife and Dave are cheering me on. Push. Push. We can see the head. Push!

Shut the fuck up. What do you think I am? A Derby Day horse that you have a bet on? I can do this. My daughter and I can do it. I know she is a daughter – we have entered the era of the ultrasound.

During this birth, everything happens in its proper order, just as it should. My daughter is born without knives or scissors, on a bright May afternoon in the Welsh valleys, with little blood and only as much pain as such an occasion deserves.

Human greatness – the greatness of being born into humanity – demands and merits pain, though God knows why. Maybe we need to remember Simone Weil's distinction between suffering and affliction (Weil, 1950). The former is creative and nurtures growth and enlightenment; the latter sets out to destroy the human within us. Affliction is the condition of mothers in concentration camps and in Sudan and Gaza. It is the condition of women with fistulas. I suffered when I gave birth to my children, but I have never been afflicted.

4.1 A Daughter's Birth

The story of Christ's maternal grandmother, St Anne, is one of the loveliest and most neglected aspects of the Marian tradition. During the Middle Ages, she was second only to her more famous daughter in the enthusiasm of her devotees. The child Jesus inhabited a matriarchal household of aunts and cousins, presided over by his grandmother and tenderly nurtured by his mother (Figure 5).

Figure 5 Master of the Holy Kinship the Younger (c. 1480-c. 1520), Altar of the Holy Kinship (c. 1480-c. 1520), Wallraf Richartz Museum, Cologne (public domain – compilation copyright held by Zenodot Verlagsgesellschaft mbH and licensed under the GNU Free Documentation Licence)

The doctrine of the Immaculate Conception is often confused with the doctrine of the Virgin Birth, but they are not the same. The Virgin Birth refers to the preservation of Mary's virginity before, during, and after Christ's birth. The Immaculate Conception refers to Mary's conception by St Anne.

The story originates from a second-century apocryphal text, *The Protevangelium of James*, which recounts Mary's life from her conception by her elderly parents, Joachim and Anna, to the slaughter of the innocents in the New Testament (Matthew 2:16–18). Anna is modelled on Hannah, Samuel's mother in the Old Testament (1 Samuel), and the story also has echoes of Anna in the Book of Tobit.

As an old man, Joachim retreats with his flocks into the desert because he has been shamed by the elders of Israel for not producing a child. This, in itself, is a startling departure from most traditional cultures in which it is the woman, not the man, who is blamed for childlessness. Anna is lamenting her double loss – her childlessness and her husband's absence – when an angel appears to Anna in her home and to Joachim in the wilderness, telling each of them that God has heard their prayer. The couple rush to meet each other at the gates of Jerusalem:

> Then, Joachim came with his flocks. Anna was standing at the gate. When she saw Joachim coming with his flocks, Anna ran and wrapped herself around his neck, saying, 'Now I know that the Lord God has blessed me greatly. See, the widow is no longer a widow and the childless woman has conceived in her womb'. (Kirby, 2025)

The Church has always taught that Mary was sexually conceived but without original sin, though theologians have disagreed as to how much pleasure the elderly couple would have derived from the act. Medieval artists had fewer inhibitions, and 'The Embrace at the Golden Gate' was a popular subject, showing a loving, erotic marital embrace. Giotto depicted this moment with exquisite tenderness – the first kiss in Western art (Figure 6; see Dragasevic, 2025).

Paintings of the birth of Mary are often confused with paintings of the nativity, but the former depict St Anne as a prosperous wife in a bedroom, surrounded by female attendants, rather than in the stable featured in images of Christ's nativity (Figure 7).

The *Protevangelium* offers a simple but moving account of Mary's birth: 'After nine months, Anna gave birth and she said to the midwife, "What is it?" The midwife said, "A girl." Anna said, "My soul exalts this day." And she put her baby to bed. After her days were completed, Anna cleansed her menstrual flow and gave her breast to the child and gave her the name Mary' (Kirby, 2025).

A mother rejoices over the birth of a daughter. Blood and milk feature in this account of childbirth. A mother names her daughter. Adam's power to name is

Figure 6 Giotto di Bondone, *Meeting at the Golden Gate* (1305), Scrovegni Chapel, Padua (Wikimedia, Creative Commons Licence)

Figure 7 Giotto di Bondone, *Birth of the Virgin* (1303–1305), Srovegni Chapel, Padua (Wikimedia Creative Commons Licence)

undone in this maternal genealogy of rejoicing and naming. Daughters are often a reason for dismay when they enter the world. They do not continue the patriarchal genealogy but are a burden until they can be married off. Is this the first moment of female redemption, its potency suppressed by a theological tradition that clings stubbornly to its patriarchal hierarchies, in defiance of the radical challenge posed by the incarnation?

Irigaray sees the symbolic rehabilitation of the mother/daughter relationship as a challenge to the patriarchal/phallocentric symbolic order, which demands the sacrifice of women's relationships to one another: 'If we are to be desired and loved by men, we must abandon our mothers, substitute for them, eliminate them in order to be *same*' (Irigaray, 1993b: 102). In such societies, 'the mother/daughter, daughter/mother relationship constitutes a highly explosive nucleus. Thinking it, and changing it, is equivalent to shaking the foundations of the patriarchal order' (Irigaray, 1994: 50).

Medieval art and devotion paid lavish attention to the role of St Anne, Jesus's grandmother. Domestic life revolved around matriarchal kinship communities, inspiring extravagant stories about St Anne, her daughters and grandchildren, central to which was the maternal flesh that gave Jesus his human body (Beattie, 2002: 155–159, 2015b). God incarnate not only had a mother, he also had a grandma.

4.2 Grandmothering

When I became a grandmother, I discovered a new devotion to St Anne. I wrote a poem, imagining her waiting through the long night of holy birth:

> Were you awake
> praying
> through the wintry night
> for your daughter
> giving birth
> to pain?
>
> Did a refrain
> of the night she was born
> play in your memory –
> your heart's delight,
> your mystery,
> your star of the sea?
>
> Did you dream
> of love's rebirth,
> earth redeemed
> and God's delight

> being born for us
> that starry night?
>
> Did you rise
> with the rising sun and,
> seeing the lily turn
> her face to the dawn,
> know that the child was born?

Research suggests that a poor or vulnerable child has a greater chance of survival if the maternal grandmother is present (Sear and Mace, 2008). From generation to generation, good mothering is a shared activity. To return to Hrdy's account, it is allomothering. She makes clear that the evolutionary process lends itself to a communal understanding of infant nurture and care. The most significant allomothers are those who are in a kinship relationship with the mother: 'As has always been true, availability of matrilineal kin – sisters, mothers, and grandmothers – makes for an especially reliable source of allomaternal assistance. Not quite a beehive, but far more valuable than a village, an extended family of matrilineal kin turns out to be a wonderful resource for rearing human infants' (Hrdy, 2000: 372).

As a grandmother to five small children, I am discovering how maternal love ripples out through generations. Some grandparents must take on the full burden of child-rearing when children are orphaned by war or sickness, or parents are unable to cope with their responsibilities. Life in sub-Saharan Africa taught me that, in many traditional cultures, grandparents have primary responsibility for young children during the first few years after weaning. This tradition has taken on a tragic dimension with the proliferation of orphaned children resulting from the HIV/AIDS pandemic. On a visit to Nairobi with the Catholic overseas aid agency, Cafod, I met some of these grandmothers and allomothers. I discovered the vital role they play in caring for sick mothers and their children.

In Catholic representations of the Holy Family, St Anne has been replaced by St Joseph, mirroring the modern nuclear family and eliding the communal significance of Christ's matriarchal kinship group. With changing gender roles and the rise in households headed by women (Trias-Prats and Esteve, 2024), the devotional and theological significance of Christ's maternal genealogy may be ripe for rehabilitation, as an expression of domestic holiness that subverts the patriarchal model of husbandly headship and wifely submission.

4.3 Continuing the Story

Thirty-eight years after our daughter was born in Wales, I was with her when she gave birth to her daughter. She planned a home delivery with a birthing bath. We bought scented candles and strings of lights to hang around the room. But as the days of waiting dragged on, the dream gave way to a harsher and more persistent reality. She was admitted to hospital and induced. Lucy Jones cautions against these birthing fantasies: 'The mythical image of "natural childbirth" is a quiet woman, surrounded by fairy lights and oils and whale sounds, peacefully and lovingly bringing a child into the world. If that is the expectation, and it doesn't go to plan, many women feel that they have failed' (2023: 68).

As my daughter struggled for hour after hour in the delivery room, I asked myself why I had colluded in the fantasy. Why did I not warn her? Perhaps we always tell ourselves that next time, it will be different. We perpetrate the subtle deceptions that ensure the survival of the human race by persuading our daughters that pregnancy, childbirth, and motherhood are blessings and gifts. They usually are, in spite of it all, but they are dark gifts threaded through with pain, sorrow, and fear. All that remained of our preparations for that serene home birth was my small statue, bought in Lourdes, of St Anne standing protectively over her little daughter (Figure 8), and now perched beside my daughter's bloodied birthing bed.

Yet there was a dance of life going on through that long birth. This is the era of high-tech medical care. My daughter was attached to a machine that monitored her heart rate and the baby's. I watched in fearful fascination as their stress levels increased with every contraction in that mutual struggle to give birth and to be born. There was an oceanic rhythm to the waves of pain and release, pain

Figure 8 Statue of St Anne and Mary

and release, each time mounting the scales of agony until, she tells me, she despaired of it ever being over.

But we are fortunate, my daughter and I. Sometimes, it is appropriate to refer to birth as a form of delivery. Modern obstetrics did indeed deliver us from the grip of Mother Nature's savage indifference to human suffering and death. My granddaughter was eventually sucked from my exhausted daughter's body by way of a ventouse extraction.

There is a passage that tells of the birth of a daughter in Toni Morrison's *Beloved* (1987). The fugitive slave Sethe gives birth in a leaky boat, fleeing from captivity, assisted by Amy, a young white woman. After the baby is safely and bloodily born, 'Amy wrapped her skirt around it and the wet sticky women clambered ashore to see what, indeed, God had in mind'. The story continues:

> Spores of bluefern growing in the hollows along the riverbank float toward the water in silver-blue lines hard to see unless you are in or near them, lying right at the river's edge when the sunshots are low and drained. Often they are mistook for insects – but they are seeds in which the whole generation sleeps confident of a future. And for a moment it is easy to believe that each one has one – will become all of what is contained in the spore: will live out its days as planned. This moment of certainty lasts no longer than that; longer, perhaps, than the spore itself.
>
> On a riverbank in the cool of a summer evening two women struggled under a shower of silvery blue. They never expected to see each other again in this world and at the moment couldn't care less. But there on a summer night surrounded by bluefern they did something together appropriately and well. A patroller passing would have sniggered to see two throw-away people, two lawless outlaws – a slave and a barefoot whitewoman with unpinned hair – wrapping a ten-minute-old baby in the rags they wore. But no patroller came and no preacher. The water sucked and swallowed itself beneath them. There was nothing to disturb them at their work. So they did it appropriately and well. (84–85)

In the unfolding of Sethe's story, that birth is a luminous and thwarted epiphany – a moment of futurity betrayed, for it is a gift that the world will refuse to allow space to grow and flourish.

Sometimes a birth can be gentle and lovely, as was the case with my daughter's birth. But birth is not about flourishing. Birth is that which a mother and child must endure to flourish beyond the struggle against futility and death.

'One does not give birth in pain, one gives birth to pain' writes Julia Kristeva (1987: 241). Natural childbirth is not the fantasy of birthing baths and home deliveries that it is made out to be. It is a struggle against the forces of death, and the mother and child do not always win. No wonder in medieval devotion and art, St Margaret, delivered from the belly of a dragon, is the patron saint of women in childbirth.

We are promised that every dying will indeed become a birthing into heaven. We must take that on trust. It is the shape of our hope, which is nothing at all like optimism. Hope is the capacity to discern love's eternity within mortality and finitude. Hope is God's Christmas gift to humankind.

5 Sacrament

26th December 1983. Our second son, our third child, is being born in Harare on Boxing Day. These fecund months have passed in a haze of contentment. We live in a country newly emerging from a bloody and divisive era of colonialism and a savage struggle for liberation. Zimbabwe was born from Rhodesia's prolonged and terrible dying. We are innocent – or perhaps wilfully ignorant? – of the new violence fermenting under Robert Mugabe's rule.

These nine months of pregnancy have been intellectually fruitful and emotionally rewarding. I have been doing an A Level in English Literature through home study. The exam was at the end of term, a couple of weeks before Christmas. I went to the local sixth form girls' school and waddled in to take my place among the astonished teenagers. A few weeks after our baby was born, I received the news that I had passed with distinction. I had taken the first small step along a path that would slowly unfold in ways beyond my wildest dreams. One cannot have it all, but a woman can be fertile and creative beyond – and sometimes instead of – childbearing.

Many years later, I published a novel about Zimbabwe's birthing pains. *Between Two Rivers* is, like all works of fiction, freighted with unconscious memories and desires, refracting life's intensities through creative imaginings that disguise their autobiographical references and distort their authorial intentions. It is a book about love and war, but somewhere in the writing, birth scripted itself into the story as love's redeeming gift to the world:

> Morag walked across the clearing. The moon had risen high in the sky so that the world seemed bathed in mother's milk. The mission lay quiet and peaceful around her, and the winter air was crystal-clear. She thought of the child in her womb and she thought of it as a whole tribe, a new human species coming into being, delicately woven together out of so many stories, so much loving, such great sadness. (Beattie, 2023: 397)

1983. Christmas night is a night of gentle labouring after that day when we celebrate the one whose birth will one day conquer death. My parents and Dave's widowed mother are staying with us in our rambling old house in Harare. Looking back, what I remember most is my father's reaction when we awoke them just after midnight and told them we were going to the hospital because I was in labour. The mothers fussed as mothers often do (we are after all so heavily invested in this regenerative process from generation to generation), but I saw a surge of emotions written on my father's face and welling up in his eyes – joy, anxiety, wonder.

Writing this evokes a memory of going to say goodnight to him when I was leaving home for the first time, to live in Paris with Dave. I was nineteen – so young, so unknowing, disguising my fear and confusion, my unnameable sorrow with a brash veneer of confidence, which is still the face I present to the world to hide that existential sadness. I wonder how much of that creative sorrow is the dark genetic gift that my father bequeathed to me, written into my DNA before and beyond all life's knocks and struggles. We are born into turbulent gene pools and unfinished stories, and these stories continue to unfold within our lives, whether we want them to or not.

That night, before I left home, my dad went to bed early. I knocked on the bedroom door and went in. He was kneeling naked beside the bed, asleep in a position of prayer. He looked so vulnerable, I felt as if my heart might break.

I knew he'd been praying for me. His spirituality meandered through poetry, music, and the rituals of Freemasonry, though he never succumbed to the strictures of religious conformity. He tried to quell his restless soul with whisky, but he had a mighty faith, and he prayed from out of the deep and the dark. His favourite hymn was 'Amazing Grace'.

That image of my naked father falling asleep over his prayers haunts me. I wrote a poem to try to exorcise the memory, but that's not how poetry works. Expression is not exorcism, but it wraps the unspeakable in words that make it almost bearable.

Baby Daddy

I found you kneeling
naked
head and elbows on the bed
drunkenly asleep at prayer
for your daughter
about to fly
away away.

Goodnight daddy.
I whispered and took flight
but now

that night
is a bruise in my heart

> when I kneel
> in prayer
>
> before a father
> whose love
> is too naked to bear.

As my mother aged into her eighties, I learned that we become mothers to our mothers, and they become our defiant and dependent octogenarian toddlers. But my father died too young to need such late-life mothering.

How strange that the attempt to remember birth brings so many memories of death and loss trailing in its wake.

5.1 Joy to the World

Christmas night, 1983. We arrive at the hospital, and I labour quietly and calmly through the early hours into the bright African dawn. I am so relaxed that I read Graham Greene's *The Comedians* from cover to cover.

Eventually, my body takes over, and once again I am consumed by the imperatives of birthing a baby. The consultant wants to give me an injection to speed things up. I'm taking up too much of his time on a bank holiday. Of course, he doesn't say that. He pretends I need it. I know I don't. I refuse and send him away. He is an irritating and unnecessary presence. The midwife is enough. I sense her stealthy delight in what I am doing, as the anarchic furies of birth take hold.

I am a wealthy white woman in Africa. Yes, by now it's postcolonial Africa, but sometimes that just means more of the same without the softening effects of colonial paternalism. This is a private hospital. The white consultant is well-paid. The African midwife is probably not, though I never thought to ask. But she likes the fact that I have told the consultant to fuck off and go and play golf. We don't need him. She and I will do this together.

I am naked. Huge belly. Ripe breasts. Sucking in life's energy and bearing down on the world to come, I have become a force of nature. I want music for this birth, so they turn on the hospital sound system. A more organised woman would have brought her own CD, but I forgot, in the flurry of entertaining the extended family for Christmas lunch. Today, women probably have Spotify playlists to help them give birth. Pause. Let me check. Yes, there it is: 'Music To Give Birth To'.

Lacking the tastefully selective algorithms of Spotify, our son enters the world to the Dance of the Sugar Plum Fairy and maternal cries of joy. Yes! Yes! Yes! Joy to the world! For this birth, there are no scissors, no stitches, no traumas. A good birth can be almost orgasmic in its joyous abandonment.

5.2 Kenosis

Male theologians have long posited an analogical relationship between divine kenosis and male orgasm. We can trace this back to the copulative philosophical relationship between inseminating form and receptive matter. Long after that has become scientifically anachronistic, the male theological establishment is still reluctant to let go of its ejaculatory intellectual wanks, its *logos spermatikos*, as expressive of divine initiative. (Dear reader, back then, when I read novels rather than theological texts, I would have wondered what on earth I was talking about. To be honest, I still do.)

Hans Urs von Balthasar expresses it more explicitly than most when he asks, 'What else is his eucharist but, at a higher level, an endless act of fruitful outpouring of his own flesh, such as a man can only achieve for a moment with a limited organ of his own body?' (1975: 150).

Never having directly experienced a male orgasm, I am willing to grant that it might feel like a cosmically kenotic experience, an emptying out of one's very being into the voracious darkness of the female flesh. That is how Balthasar describes it, in a chapter titled 'Conquest of the Bride' in his book *Heart of the World*. He indulges a lurid sado-masochistic fantasy of the wedding night between Christ and the Church as a metaphor for the incarnation:

> I surrendered to the temptation of ... delivering myself up to the obscure chaos of a body, of plunging below the shiny surface of the flesh; the temptation of passing over into this world – this simmering darkness, opposed to the Father's light. ... I dared to enter the body of my Church, the deadly body which you are ... But I have defeated you through weakness and my Spirit has overpowered my unruly and recalcitrant flesh. (Never has woman made more desperate resistance!) (1979: 196)

Here is the masculine theological imaginary, reversing the process of birth, individuation, and separation, undoing the purity and rationality of form, to plunge into the bloody chaos of the body from which he came, the body that provided him with his first home and birthed him into life. He goes there with murderous intent – to conquer that body once and for all, to overpower and defeat it, to end forever its viscous capacity to swamp the light of the Father with its fleshy seductions.

Not all theological fantasies move in this direction of the flesh. If, for Balthasar, the Eucharistic celebration of the incarnation morphs into a kenotic sex act of rape and conquest, for many of the Catholic Church's bishops, it would seem to offer an escape from the messy materiality of being to an eternal transcendence of spirit. This is what I conclude from a document prepared for the 2005 Synod of Bishops on 'The Eucharist: Source and Summit of the Life and Mission of the Church'. The document quotes John Chrysostom, Sermon III, *De Sacerdotio*:

> For when you see the Lord sacrificed, laid upon the altar, and the priest standing and praying over the victim, and all the worshippers empurpled with that precious blood, can you then think that you are still among men, and standing upon the earth? Are you not, on the contrary, straightway translated to heaven, and casting out every carnal thought from the soul, do you not, with disembodied spirit and pure reason, contemplate the things which are in heaven? (Synod of Bishops, 2004)

Kenosis, birth, transcendence, disembodiment – the perpetual struggle of the masculine imaginary against the flesh – a struggle that takes the form of violent and bloody conquest or rationalised abstraction. No wonder Western culture is riven today between the idolatry of scientific rationalism on the one hand, and the bloody madness of military intervention and state-sanctioned violence on the other.

Yet what of the kenosis of birth? What of the maternal body that empties itself in the giving of life, in the blood and water of childbirth? This is my body, given for you. This is my blood, spilled out for you.

5.3 The Birth of Christ

Catholic doctrine teaches that Mary suffered no pain in childbirth and that she remained a virgin before, during, and after childbirth. The term 'ever-virgin' (*aeiparthenos*) was used in the emergent Marian devotions of the early Church. For modern feminists, this painless virginal birth is an affront to women, seen as yet another example of the Catholic hierarchy's attempt to suppress and control female sexuality and the bodily processes that go with it.

Perhaps the virgin birth is an expression of that ancient and modern male fantasy, men's enduring attempt to transcend and deny the raw fact that we enter the world through the birth canal by way of a woman's vagina, coated in vernix, squashed with the pressure of her pelvis, born in the blood and water that flow from her womb. Surely, God's gateway into the human condition was an altogether purer and more bloodless affair?

Mumford refers to the indignation of Pliny the Elder, writing in his *Natural History* of the humiliation of birth and infant dependency:

> But man alone on the day of his birth Nature casts away naked on the naked ground, to burst at once into wailing and weeping, and none among all the animals is more prone to tears, and that immediately at the very beginning of life ... This initiation into the light is followed by a period of bondage such as befalls not even the animals bred in our midst, fettering all his limbs; and thus

when successfully born he lies with hands and feet in shackles, weeping – the animal that is to lord it over all the rest. (Mumford, 2013: 111, quoting Pliny)

Early Christian thinkers understood this philosophical revulsion over maternal origins. They made it part of the glorious scandal of the divinity of Christ that he was born of a woman – his divinity attested to by Mary's virginity, his humanity attested to by Mary's motherhood (Beattie, 2007).

Against the abstract perfection of the Greek divine, protected from and insulated against the corruption of the flesh associated with the maternal body and death, Christianity worshipped a God born of a woman and crucified on a cross. St Augustine beautifully expresses the challenge that the incarnation poses to abstract philosophical concepts of divinity and truth:

> *Truth has sprung from the earth, and Justice has looked forth from heaven* (Psalm 84:12). Truth, which is *the bosom of the Father* (John 1:18), has sprung from the earth, in order also to be in the bosom of his mother. Truth, by which the world is held together, has sprung from the earth, in order to be carried in a woman's arms. Truth, on which the bliss of the angels is incorruptibly nourished, has sprung from the earth, in order to be suckled at breasts of flesh. Truth, which heaven is not big enough to hold, has sprung from the earth, in order to be placed in a manger. (Augustine, 1993: 21)

Writing in the early third century, Tertullian refutes Marcion and others who would deny the reality of the incarnation by giving a visceral account of Christ's birth that is unique among surviving writings on Mary's maternity. He argues that 'there is no nativity without flesh, and no flesh without nativity':

> Come now, beginning from the nativity itself, declaim against the uncleanness of the generative elements within the womb, the filthy concretion of fluid and blood, of the growth of the flesh for nine months long out of that very mire. Describe the womb as it enlarges from day to day, – heavy, troublesome, restless even in sleep, changeful in its feelings of dislike and desire. Inveigh now likewise against the shame itself of a woman in travail, which, however, ought rather to be honoured in consideration of that peril, or to be held sacred in respect of (the mystery of) nature. Of course you are horrified also at the infant, which is shed into life with the embarrassments which accompany it from the womb; you likewise, of course, loathe it even after it is washed, when it is dressed out in its swaddling-clothes, graced with repeated anointing, smiled on with nurse's fawns. This reverend course of nature, you, O Marcion, (are pleased to) spit upon; and yet, in what way you were born? You detest a human being at his birth; then after what fashion do you love anybody? ... Well, then, loving man [Christ] loved his nativity also, and his flesh as well. (Tertullian, 1885)

Tertullian's description has long been overlaid by more ascetic versions of the divine birth. I argue here, against Tertullian, though not without appreciating his description, that there is theological coherence to the doctrine of the virgin birth, if we understand that Eve/Mary constitute the existential and eschatological dimensions of womanhood (Beattie, 2002). Like all the core doctrines of the Catholic faith, I believe that these Marian mysteries invite reflection and reinterpretation, lest we strip away all that does not lend itself to rational justification and are left with only the husk of faith (see Spretnak, 2004). That is why, in my research and writings on Mary, I've asked what these doctrines might mean in terms of the redemption of women and the sacramental significance of the female body. So, let me revisit those Marian traditions with that question in mind.

5.4 Redeeming Mary

Mary is traditionally known as the New Eve. This is often interpreted in dualistic language that opposes virginity, obedience, and life to seduction, disobedience, and death. There are, however, different interpretations to be excavated from neglected aspects of the Marian tradition. Sometimes, to move forward, we must retrieve what has been neglected or forgotten along the way.

As the first woman of the new creation in Christ, Mary represents the redemption of Eve and her liberation from the consequences of Genesis – pain in childbirth and domination in marriage. Christ does no violence to any body, least of all to the maternal body that bore him into the world. We must look to Calvary to see the redemption and transformation of birth, but I shall return to that.

Mary's virginity breaks the cycle of sex and death within which we find ourselves. It is not the end of sex, but the end of sexual proprietorship and domination. As the husband of the Virgin and adoptive father of Christ, Joseph constitutes a challenge to patriarchal concepts of masculinity, marriage, and fatherhood that the Church has yet to fully embrace.

The fulfilment of the prophecy made to the woman in Genesis, that she will become 'mother of all the living' (Genesis 3:20), is not just about the healing of human relationships, but about the redemption and renewal of all creation. St Anselm's prayer to Mary gives lavish expression to what this new creation means:

> O woman full and overflowing with grace,
> plenty flows from you
> to make all creatures green again.

> O virgin blessed and ever blessed,
> whose blessing is upon all nature,
> not only is the creature blessed by the Creator,
> but the Creator is blessed by the creature too ...
> O truly, 'the Lord is with you',
> to whom the Lord gave himself,
> that all nature in you might be in him.
>
> (Anselm, 1973: 120–121)

Mary's sinless female body is the beginning of the new creation, the virgin matter (earth/mother) from whom the new Adam is born.

Patristic theologians repeatedly insisted upon the significance of Mary for the redemption of women, as in a homily attributed to St Augustine:

> For this cause did the Virgin Mary undertake all those functions of nature (conceiving, bringing forth, giving milk), with regard to Our Lord Jesus Christ, that she might succour all women who fly to her protection, and thus restore the whole race of women as the New Eve, even as the New Adam, the Lord Jesus Christ, repaired the whole race of men. (Attributed to Augustine, Sermon 15, quoted in Beattie, 2007)

But this does not mean a life of eschatological bliss. On the contrary, Mary walks the most rugged path of maternal sorrow and loss. She carries within her own heart the piercings that every maternal heart endures in the lifelong struggle to love and let go (Luke 2:35). There is no love without sorrow, and the more we love, the more we suffer.

Like so many women in today's world, Mary gave birth far from home in harsh conditions, made to conform to the bureaucratic diktats of a census that then and now reduces the flesh and blood vulnerabilities of life to abstractions and numbers. She experienced the plight of the refugee, fleeing in horror from the violence that Herod unleashed upon the male toddlers of the women she had grown up amongst – her friends, cousins, and playmates. These are aspects of her life that require no leap of faith. As the *Mater Dolorosa* at the foot of the cross, Mary embodies the fullness of maternal love and mourning. But let's return to the Marian mysteries, those which ask us to trust what we cannot rationally explain, and to make doctrine a doorway to prayer that seeks the redemptive mystery concealed within the improbable story.

5.5 Redeeming Motherhood

The virgin birth, the perpetual virginity of Mary, and the doctrine of her sinlessness can all be reclaimed as signs of hope for women who labour under the historical burdens of patriarchal domination and maternal distress. In the foregoing sections, I have excavated and explored themes of guilt and inadequacy, failure and shame, affliction and death, which cling to the underbelly of the maternal romance perpetuated by popes and patriarchs. Maternal guilt and sorrow are symptoms of suffering love, of perfect love's inadequacy in the face of life's harsh struggles. We grieve because we love, and we blame ourselves because we want our beloved children to have mothers who are not only good enough, but perfect in every way. The fantasised ideal devalues the quotidian endeavours of maternal life, casting a pall of insufficiency over every inconspicuous act of love that weaves us into the enduring resilience of the human spirit. We rise to life's challenges sometimes in spite of, and sometimes because of, the parenting we received, and our children will be the same.

The doctrine of Mary's sinlessness is consolation for the lamentations of guilt and failure that run through the story I'm telling here. When our children suffer, we mothers blame ourselves. When they fail to model the kind of lives we had hoped for them, we ask where we failed. When they fall into trouble with the authorities, rebel against our religious and social conventions, hang out with the wrong kind of people, we feel reinforced in our sense that we must have been bad mothers. These struggles are intensified by consumerism and its commodification of the nuclear family, for few women can match up to the images projected by the advertising industry and purveyors of the religious status quo.

Mary was what every mother yearns to be – the perfect mother of the perfect child. Yet she shares all the griefs and anxieties of maternal life, even though she is full of grace, sinless, and chosen by God. There is a tragic thread woven through time, and it is gathered in and knotted around the body on the cross. The mother at the foot of the cross shares her child's torments, but there is no guilt attached to her suffering. Her maternal tears are the pure distillation of sorrow, and in her we, too, can learn to suffer without guilt, to mourn without shame.

The Christian story is not an exhortation to moral perfection under threat of divine punishment (though that is how it has been told, especially concerning the female sex). It is not a pat on the head for the bourgeois wife smugly parading her well-behaved children into church every Sunday. It is hope and consolation amid humanity's often tragic and catastrophic failures, so many of which have been presided over by tyrannical and violent oedipal gods, including the god of much Christian theology and devotion.

The story of God incarnate, born of a woman, is a vocation to hope, to trust, and to love through the chaos and frustration of life. For women, the myth of Genesis explains this in terms of the gendered sufferings of marital domination and childbirth, but in Mary, the New Eve, this becomes a story of redeeming love amidst the desolation and abandonment of Eden betrayed.

5.6 Birthing Christ

Let me play with a thought experiment that is not entirely without precedent in the Catholic tradition. I am borrowing extensively here from my essay, 'Gendering Genesis, Engendering Difference: A Catholic Theological Quest' (2016a).

The sexual metaphor of kenosis to which I referred earlier may not be entirely inappropriate, but it is incomplete. It taps into that ancient tradition of the *logos spermatikos* – the inseminating Word – but behind that philosophical term lurks a hidden world of symbolic and sacramental associations with birth. For if, on the cross, some see a sign of phallic insemination, must there not also be a vagina, if new life is to be born out of death?

There is a peculiar era in Christian art between the twelfth and fourteenth centuries, during which Christ's torso appears as a phallus, as seen in numerous crucifixes from this period (Figures 9 and 10). If we look more closely, we see that the wound in his side is spurting the body fluids of blood and water in the direction of his mother at the foot of the cross. These are birth fluids – water and

Figure 9 Unknown Master, *Crucifixion* (1265–1270) Louvre Museum (public domain, via Wikimedia Commons)

A Theology of Becoming

Figure 10 Master of the Berthold Sacramentary, *Weingarten Missal* (c. 1216) The Morgan Library and Museum (public domain, via Wikimedia Commons)

blood gush from bodies in childbirth, not in death. These signify the birth of the Church – the New Eve, personified in Mary – and baptismal rebirth. 'Unless you are born again, you can never enter the Kingdom of Heaven', Jesus tells Nicodemus (John 3:3).

Caroline Walker Bynum writes: 'Medieval hymns and sermons had long stressed that all birth is in blood. ... By the fourteenth and fifteenth centuries, not only is Christ understood to be born and born anew in blood; he himself gives birth. The blood of the passion is the blood of birthing. Hence the fertile, separated blood from Christ's side is female blood' (Bynum, 2007: 159).

The wound in Christ's side was commonly described in terms of the birthing maternal body in patristic and medieval theology, with Christ giving birth to the Church in the same way that Eve was 'birthed' from the side of Adam (Bynum, 2007; Miller, 2013). In medieval art, the wound is sometimes explicitly represented as a vulva (Figure 11).

Such imagery suggests that Christ impregnates his own body to give birth to the maternal Church, in whom his body and blood will henceforth become food for the life of the world. I am tempted to push this even further to suggest that,

Figure 11 Jean Le Noir, *Christ's Side Wound, Psalter of Bonne de Luxembourg* (c. 1349) (public domain, via Wikimedia Commons

just as Christ was conceived in the virgin body of Mary, so the Church as the New Eve is conceived in the virgin body of Christ. These symbolic associations have a cataphatic capacity to open the sacramental imagination to a proliferation of resonances and analogies – bearing in mind that analogical affirmation teeters on the brink of negation and must therefore not be taken too literally or pushed too far. The alienated sexual couple of Genesis is reconciled in the body of the crucified Christ. This self-fecundating, polymorphous body redeems the human by experiencing in its flesh the agonies of birth and death, becoming one flesh with the mother in a consummation of desire that goes far beyond the Freudian myth and the incest taboo.

On Calvary, Mary/Eve sees the taking on of the wounds of birth so that her female flesh might be healed, redeemed, and renewed. She participates in this redemption in an inversion of those theological fantasies of male disembodiment and female carnality. Christ is the carnal body, the one who bleeds and cries out and shits and dies as his body is torn apart so that life might be born. The woman is the one who feels her spirit plunging into his flesh, her heart pierced through with the piercing of his body.

As long as the ordained priesthood remains tethered to the idea of essential biological maleness, the rich fecundity of new life in Christ cannot find full sacramental expression in the Eucharist. As I write this, a woman has been appointed as the new Archbishop of Canterbury. Before ordination, Sarah Mullally was a nurse and midwife. I find myself imagining the priest as midwife to Christ on the birthing bed of the cross. The ordination of women is not about rights or equality. It is about opening the sacramental imagination to the fullness of redemption for all creation, including humankind created male and female in the image of God.

5.7 Towards a Beginning

I have acknowledged my debt to James Mumford for providing the stimulus for writing this. His phenomenology of maternal life is written from the perspective of the male outsider, whose sense of self is untouched by the otherness he observes. What would happen if the dynamic capacities and shifting identities of the maternal body became normative in the construction of the person? What if the incarnation reconstitutes the masculine subject as the maternal other of the symbolic order, inviting a radically counter-cultural alternative to the patriarchal and androcentric status quo?

Recent popes have made much of the idea that the Church is a woman, which is not in itself a new claim but has gained new ideological currency as an argument against women priests (Beattie, 2016a and 2016b). This is accompanied by the claim that the feminine metaphors of bride, virgin, and mother applied to the Church also apply to all members of the Church, male and female, beyond the essential maleness of the sacramental priesthood. So, what would happen if baptismal rebirth incorporated the male subject into refigurations of self and other, based not on masculine identity but on the female otherness of bodiliness, relationality, and the capacity to give birth to another? I conclude with those questions.

6 Redeeming Birth

> Jesus replied, 'Very truly I tell you, no one can see the kingdom of God unless they are born again'. 'How can someone be born when they are old?' Nicodemus asked. 'Surely they cannot enter a second time into their mother's womb to be born!' Jesus answered, 'Very truly I tell you, no one can enter the kingdom of God unless they

are born of water and the Spirit. Flesh gives birth to flesh, but the Spirit gives birth to spirit. You should not be surprised at my saying, "You must be born again."'

(John 3: 3–5)

'He can no longer have God for his Father, who has not the Church for his mother'

(Cyprian, 2002: 4)

Yahweh advances like a hero, like a warrior he rouses his fire. He shouts, he raises the war cry, he shows his might against his foes. For a long time I have been silent, I have kept quiet, held myself in check, groaning like a woman in labour, panting and gasping for air.

(Isaiah 42: 14–15)

The Christian theological tradition has been corrupted time and again by the idolatry of a warrior God who sows violence, destruction, and conquest in His wake. It has muffled the groans and cries of God labouring to be born anew in the trinitarian relationality of the three-in-one in whose image we are made. The subject of Christian theology, a Feuerbachian projection of the One God, is yet to be born again in the image and likeness of the Trinity – this God whose oneness is constituted by otherness.

Yet throughout the tradition, there have been glimmers of God giving birth to God in the dynamic processions of divine being as a verb, not a noun. We might say that God's being is an eternal becoming and emerging, so long as we are mindful that we are talking nonsense when we apply our human categories and descriptions to the source and telos of love beyond all naming.

6.1 Trinitarian Rebirth

There are abundant references to the maternal Trinity in Christian devotional writings, most famously perhaps in Julian of Norwich's *Revelations of Divine Love* (1998). In the seventh century, the Council of Toledo used the language of the unceasing becoming of the Son 'from the womb of the Father' (Fordham University, 2025). Through the ages, theologians have performed linguistic contortions to explain how this mothering God is really a Father, in what Mary Daly calls the 'sacred House of Mirrors', presided over by 'anointed Male Mothers, who naturally are called Fathers' (Daly, 1986: 195). There is much more to say on how trinitarian analogies of birthing and generation can be reclaimed and reinterpreted, and I explore these in some detail elsewhere (Beattie, 2013: Chapter 18, 'The Maternal Trinity'). For now, let me sketch a proposal that requires fleshing out, if the male theological subject is to be reborn as the fleshy becoming self, made in the image of the incarnate, birthing God.

What follows would benefit from engagement with Christine Battersby's book, *The Phenomenal Woman: Feminist Metaphysics and the Patterns of*

Identity (1998), in which she deconstructs the normative masculine subject of modern ethics by proposing an alternative model of normativity informed by the female body with its childbearing capacities: 'I am asking what happens if we model personal and individual identity in terms of the female. Rather than treating women as somehow exceptional, I start from the question of what would have to change were we to take seriously the notion that a "person" could normally, at least always potentially, become two?' (1998: 2). The male reader of Battersby's book must deconstruct his subject position to move into the dynamic fluidity of the maternal self who changes over time.

While Battersby's philosophy offers no engagement with theology, her book would be a rich resource for rethinking what kind of transformation is entailed when the masculinised subject of the social order is baptismally reborn. Baptism heals the primal wound of alienation by offering a symbolics of rebirth from the maternal body of the Church.

Battersby argues that 'the ontological dependence of the foetus on the mother' and the fact that women are culturally conditioned to be primary carers for children, means that questions of power, dependence, and relationality position the female subject in a more fundamental way than questions of equality and autonomy: 'For the (normalized) "woman", society is not ever – not even ideally – a collection of equals'. The self predicated metaphorically upon the birthing body 'does not emerge out of the exclusion or abjection of the "other" ... Instead, it is from intersecting force-fields that "self" and "other" emerge' (1998: 8). This makes the thinking of identity a quest to discern 'a pattern of relationships, and an interweaving with otherness', analogous to 'a world of sound and music' (1998: 9). This could open into a rich theological anthropology shaped by the understanding that to be made in the image of God is for the baptised to be essentially relational, to acquire an identity constituted by the trinitarian interweaving of otherness. It invites reflection on Battersby's argument that the 'embodied, fleshy self' of the female invites an understanding of self and other in a fluid relationship of emergence and mutability, which invites 'a metaphysics of becoming' (1998: 11).

Battersby writes:

> Recognizing natality – the *conceptual* link between the paradigm 'woman' and the body that births – does not imply that all women either can or 'should' give birth. Instead, an emphasis on natality as an abstract category of embodied (female) selves means that we need to rethink identity. The 'self' is not a fixed, permanent or pre-given 'thing' or 'substance' that undergoes metamorphosis, but that nevertheless remains always unaltered through change. Instead, we need to think of identity as emerging out of a play of relationships and force-fields that together constitute the horizons of

a (shared) space-time. We need a metaphysics of fluidity and mobile relationships; not a metaphysics of fixity, or even of flexibility. However, that metaphysics must also be able to explain how a subject might be scored by relationality into uniqueness. (1998: 7)

This offers a vital insight into how the fleshy fluidity of the incarnate and resurrected Christ might offer a lens through which to ask what it means to be a person who is continuously becoming and emerging as a 'metaphysical amphibian' (Stump, 2003: 36) between worlds, yearning for the (m)othering God incarnate in Mary's child.

6.2 The Reborn Self

The autonomous individual, modelled on the One of monotheism, is birthed anew in baptismal water and blood to become a person made in the relational image of the dynamic, eternal becoming of the Trinity. This is not an act of isolated individualism (though it risks becoming that in some Protestant theologies), but an incorporation into the communal, maternal body of the Church. This has profound ecclesiological implications, especially when we apply Battersby's phenomenology to Rachel Muer's suggestion that the pregnant body serves as a potent metaphor for exploring what it means to be part of the body of the Church.

Muers argues that the biblical authors invite us to read scripture from within the body, and this opens up the texts to multiple readings:

> Reading these texts from a pregnant body disturbs one set of obvious interpretations – and sets other interpretations going that can affect both how we read bodies and how we read church communities. Pregnancy makes a different kind of sense of how the parts of a body work together; it makes a different kind of sense of a body's coherence and stability over time; and it makes a different kind of sense of the boundaries of the body, what counts as a 'part' or not a 'part' of this whole. (Muers, 2024: 36)

I began this Element with a reference to Derridean ideas of *différance* as the dangerous supplement that destabilises meaning, through textual hauntings of absence and otherness associated with the mother and nature. With this in mind, I would extend Muer's ideas to include all the ways in which scripture is inhabited and lived in the material performativity of everyday life and sacramental worship, beyond reading. My work with African communities has made me aware that literacy is a relatively new phenomenon and still not universally accessible. At least until the Reformation and the invention of the printing press, reading scripture was the prerogative of an educated elite who controlled access and interpretation. Most Christians heard and saw scripture in preaching and the visual arts rather than through reading. As the art of reading yields to new forms of communication enabled by online technology, vital questions arise about how Christians inhabit and express the ecclesial body constituted by scripture and sacramental presence.

To develop these questions in dialogue with Battersby and Muers would require another book. It would entail a fluidity of imaginative positioning of the self as both the pregnant body and the child in the womb. In Catholic ecclesiology and ethics, the Christian belongs within the womb of the Marian Church and is called to a maternal ethos of care for the vulnerable as an expression of God's sustaining love for the world. In her study of the maternal ecclesiology of the early Church, Cristina Lledo Gomez examines how these two perspectives were integrated, situating Christians as both under the maternal protection of Mary and as adults called to mother others: 'The Catholic maxim applies: it is not "either/or" but "both/and"' (2018: 1. See also Cunneen, 1991).

The language of baptism clothes the naked human animal with trinitarian personhood. Theology springing from the graced creativity of contemplation opens our imaginations to the myriad possibilities of gendered loving and being that stream between the sexual poles of reproductive necessity. Christian personhood is situated in the space of encounter between the infinity of love and the finitude of the law, and the promise of eternal life shines through the gaps in the vulnerable and suffering finitude of the mortal body in time and space.

Through the transgressive potency of sacramental life, we find ourselves at play with God. In this space where hope and desolation together form the shadow dance of the Christian soul, the wounded orphan of the Freudian psyche calls out to the Mother of God in prayer and not in despair, in a language of *jouissance* laden with insatiable longings for wholeness and peace:

> Hail, our queen, mother of mercy, our life, our sweetness and our hope.
> We cry to you, exiles as we are,
> children of Eve;
> we sigh to you, groaning and weeping
> in this valley of tears.
> Ah then, our intercessor, turn your eyes—your merciful eyes—upon us.
> And after this exile is over
> show to us Jesus, blessed fruit of your womb.
> O merciful, O holy, O sweet virgin Mary.

References

Anselm (1973). *The Prayers and Meditations of St Anselm*. Translated by Benedicta Ward. London: Penguin Books.

Aubel, Judi (2021). Grandmothers – A Neglected Family Resource for Saving Newborn Lives. *BMJ Global Health* 6: 4003808. https://doi.org/10.1136/bmjgh-2020–003808.

Augustine, Sermon 185 and Sermon 215 (1993). John E. Rotelle OSA, ed., *The Works of Saint Augustine: A Translation for the 21st Century*. 'Sermons'. III/6. Translated by Edmund Hill OP. New Rochelle, NY: New City Press.

Balthasar, Hans Urs von (1975). *Elucidations*. Translated by John Riches. London: SPCK.

⸺ (1979). *Heart of the World*. Translated by Erasmo S. Leiva. San Francisco: Ignatius Press.

Barth, Karl (1960). The Basic Form of Humanity. *Church Dogmatics* III.2 (1948). Translated by GW Bromiley and TF Torrance. Edinburgh: T&T Clark, pp. 222–84.

Basset, Lytta (2007). *Holy Anger: Jacob, Job, Jesus*. London: Continuum.

Battersby, Christine (1998). *The Phenomenal Woman: Feminist Metaphysics and the Patterns of Identity*. Cambridge, MA: Polity Press.

Beattie, Tina (2023). *Between Two Rivers*. Rye: Christabel Press.

⸺ (2016a). Gendering Genesis, Engendering Difference: A Catholic Theological Quest. *Svensk Teologisk Kvartalscrift*. Årg. 92: 102–17.

⸺ (2016b). Repairing the Sacred Canopy – A Reflection on the Symbolic Anthropology of Church Documents from the Council to *Mulieris Dignitatem*. Marinella Perroni and Hervé Legrand, eds., *We Have Something to Say: Theologians Re-read Vatican II*. Edizioni Paoline, Rome, Saggistica series.

⸺ (2015a). Dignity Beyond Rights: Human Development in the Context of the Capabilities Approach and Catholic Social Teaching. *Australian eJournal of Theology* 22(3): 150–165.

⸺ (2015b). Saint Anne: A Saint for Today? – A Reflection on Grandmothers and Holy Families. In Catholic Women Speak Network eds., *Catholic Women Speak: Bringing Our Gifts to the Table*. Mahwah NJ: Paulist Press, pp. 70–74.

⸺ (2014). Whose Rights? – Which Rights? – The United Nations, the Vatican, Gender and Sexual and Reproductive Rights. *Heythrop Journal* 55(6): 1080–1090. https://doi.org/10.1111/heyj.12205.

(2013). *Theology After Postmodernity: Divining the Void – a Lacanian reading of Thomas Aquinas*. Oxford: Oxford University Press.

(2009). Catholicism, Choice and Consciousness: A Feminist Theological Perspective on Abortion. *International Journal of Public Theology* 4(1): 51–75. https://doi.org/10.1163/187251710X12578338897863.

(2007). Mary in Patristic Theology. In Sarah Jane Boss ed., *Mary: The Complete Resource*. London and New York: Continuum, pp. 75–105.

(2006). *New Catholic Feminism: Theology and Theory*. London: Routledge.

(2002). *God's Mother, Eve's Advocate*. London: Continuum.

Biblical quotations are from the *New International Version (UK)* (2011). Bible Gateway Website. www.biblegateway.com/versions/New-International-Version-UK-NIVUK-Bible/.

Bildhauer, Bettina (2013). Medieval European Conceptions of blood: truth and human integrity. *The Journal of the Royal Anthropological Institute*: S57–S76. https://doi.org/10.1111/1467-9655.12016.

Buber, Martin (1958). *I and Thou*. Translated by Ronald Gregor Smith. New York: Charles Scribner's Sons.

Bynum, Caroline Walker (2007). *Wonderful Blood: Theology and Practice in Late Medieval Northern Germany and Beyond*. Philadelphia: University of Pennsylvania Press.

Campbell, Olivia (2019). The Rebirth of Placenta Rituals. *Sapiens*, 9 May. www.sapiens.org/biology/placenta/.

CIA.gov (2025). Maternal Mortality Ratio. *The World Factbook*. www.cia.gov/the-world-factbook/field/maternal-mortality-ratio/country-comparison/.

Cixous, Hélène Cixous (1976). The Laugh of the Medusa. Translated by Keith Cohen and Paula Cohen. *Signs: Journal of Women in Culture and Society* 1(4): 875–893.

Cullinan, Colleen Carpenter. (2008). In Pain and Sorrow: Childbirth, Incarnation, and the Suffering of Women. *Cross Currents* 58(1): 95–107. https://doi.org/10.1111/j.1939-3881.2008.00006.x.

Cunneen, Sally (1991). *Mother Church: What the Experience of Women Is Teaching Her*. Mahwah, NJ: Paulist Press.

Cunningham, David S. (2003). What Do We Mean by 'God'? In William C. Placher, ed., *Essentials of Christian Theology*. Louisville, Kentucky: Westminster John Knox Press, pp. 76–92.

Curry, Gwenetta (2023). Black Women's Maternal Health in the US and UK. Abstract of Paper given at 17th World Congress on Public Health, May 2–6, 2023, Rome. *Population Medicine* 5(Supplement): A1386, p. 403. https://doi.org/10.18332/popmed/164353.

Cyprian (2002). *Treatise on the Unity of the* Church. Ebook. Blackmask Online. www.blackmask.com.

Daly, Mary (1990). *Gyn/Ecology: The Metaethics of Radical Feminism*. Boston: Beacon Press.

Daly, Mary (1986). *Beyond God the Father: Towards a Philosophy of Women's Liberation*. London: The Women's Press.

Derrida, Jacques (1976). *Of Grammatology*. Translated by Gayatri Chakravorty Spivak. Baltimore MD: John Hopkins University Press.

Dragasevic, Petra (2025). The First Kiss in Art History. *Daily Art Magazine*, 10 July. www.dailyartmagazine.com/giotto-meeting-at-the-golden-gate/.

Erikson, Erik (1994). *Insight and Responsibility: Lectures on the Ethical Implications of Psychoanalytic Insight*. London: W.W. Norton.

Fordham University (2025). 11th Council of Toledo: Symbol of Faith (675). *Internet Medieval Sourcebook*. sourcebooks.fordham.edu/source/675Council oftoledo-creed.asp.

Francis, Pope (2013). Apostolic Exhortation: *Evangelii Gaudium*. www.vati can.va/content/francesco/en/apost_exhortations/documents/papa-frances co_esortazione-ap_20131124_evangelii-gaudium.html.

Gomez, Cristina Lledo (2018). *The Church As Woman and Mother*. Mahwah, NJ: Paulist Press.

Grady, Denise (2014). The Mysterious Tree of a Newborn's Life: The Push to Understand the Placenta. *The New York Times*, July 14. https://www.nytimes.com/2014/07/15/health/the-push-to-understand-the-placenta.html?smid=url-share.

Gremmels, Becket, Peter J. Cataldo, Elliott Louis Bedford, and Cornelia R. Graves (2014). The Metaphysical Status of the Placenta. *The National Catholic Bioethics Quarterly* 14(2): 295–333. https://doi.org/10.5840/ncbq201414231.

Hahn, Michael and Shahan, Lydia (2024). Pregnancy, Motherhood and Mysticism: Reading the Texts of Angela of Foligno. In Karen O'Donnell and Claire Williams eds., *Pregnancy and Birth: Critical Theological Conceptions*. Kindle Edition, London: SCM Press. pp. 201–221.

Hrdy, Sarah Blaffer (2009). *Mothers and Others: The Evolutionary Origins of Mutual Understanding*. Cambridge, MA: Harvard University Press.

(2000). *Mother Nature: Maternal Instincts and How They Shape the Human Species*. London: Vintage.

Irigaray, Luce (2013). Toward a Mutual Hospitality. In Thomas Claviez ed., *Conditions of Hospitality: Ethics, Politics, and Aesthetics on the Threshold of the Possible*. Bronx, NY: Fordham University Press, pp. 42–54.

(2008). *Sharing the World*. London: Continuum.

(1994). Women-Mothers, the Silent Substratum of the Social Order. Translated by David Macey. In Margaret Whitford, ed. Oxford: Blackwell Publishers, pp. 47–52.

(1993a). *Sexes and Genealogies*. Translated by Gillian C. Gill. New York: Columbia University Press.

(1993b). *An Ethics of Sexual Difference*. Translated by Carolyn Burke and Gillian C. Gill. London: The Athlone Press.

Jolly, Hugh (1975). *Book of Child Care: Complete Guide for Today's Parents*. London: Allen and Unwin.

Jones, Lucy (2023). *Matrescence: On the Metamorphosis of Pregnancy, Childbirth and Motherhood*. London: Penguin Books. Kindle Edition.

Julian of Norwich (1998). *Revelations of Divine Love*. Translated by Elizabeth Spearing. London: Penguin Books.

Kamitsuka, Margaret D. (2024a). *Desirable Belief: A Theology of Eros*. Minneapolis, MN: Fortress Press.

Kamitsuka, Margaret D. (2024b). The Precarity and Moral Obligations of Pregnancy. In Karen O'Donnell and Claire Williams eds., *Pregnancy and Birth: Critical Theological Conceptions*. Kindle Edition London: SCM Press. pp. 340–358.

Kirby, Peter (2025). Infancy Gospel of James. Translated by Shelly Matthews. *Early Christian Writings*. www.earlychristianwritings.com/text/infancy james-hock.html.

Kirsch, Adam (2018). Black Fire on White Fire. *Jewish Review of Books*. jewishreviewofbooks.com/articles/2925/black-fire-white-fire/#.

Kristeva, Julia (1987). *Tales of Love*. Translated by Leon S. Roudiez. New York: Columbia University Press.

(1982). *Powers of Horror: An Essay on Abjection*. Translated by Leon S. Roudiez. New York: Columbia University Press.

(1980). Motherhood According to Giovanni Bellini. In Leon S. Roudiez, ed., *Desire in Language: A Semiotic Approach to Literature and Art*. New York: Columbia University Press, pp. 237–270.

Kristof, Nicholas D. and WuDunn, Sheryl (2010). *Half the Sky: How to Change the World*. London: Virago Press.

Lacan, Jacques (1983). God and the *Jouissance* of The Woman (1972–1973). In Juliet Mitchell and Jacqueline Rose eds., *Feminine Sexuality: Jacques Lacan and the École Freudienne*. Basingstoke: Macmillan Press, pp. 137–48.

Laqueur, Thomas (1990). *Making Sex: Body and Gender from the Greeks to Freud*. Cambridge, MA: Harvard University Press.

Leach, Penelope (1977). *Your Baby and Child: From Birth to Age Five*. London: Michael Joseph.

References

Levinas, Emmanuel (1989). Martin Buber and the theory of knowledge (written in 1958, first published, in German, in 1963). In Sean Hand, ed., *The Levinas Reader*, ed. Sean Hand. Oxford, Blackwell, pp. 59–74.

Liedloff, Jean (1975). *The Continuum Concept: In Search of Happiness Lost*. London: Arkana.

McDonald, Chine (2025). *Unmaking Mary: Shattering the Myth of Perfect Motherhood*. London: Hodder and Stoughton.

Merleau-Ponty, Maurice (1962). *Phenomenology of Perception*. Translated by Colin Smith. London: Routledge.

Miller, Sarah Alison (2013). *Medieval Monstrosity and the Female Body*. London: Routledge.

Morrison, Toni (1987). *Beloved*. New York: Knopf.

Muers, Rachel (2024). The Body Is (Not Quite) One. In Karen O'Donnell and Claire Williams, eds., *Pregnancy and Birth: Critical Theological Conceptions*. London: SCM Press. Kindle Edition, pp. 34–52.

Mumford, James (2013). *Ethics at the Beginning of Life: A Phenomenological Critique*. Oxford: Oxford University Press.

National Health Service (2025). Rhesus Disease. www.nhs.uk/conditions/rhesus-disease/.

O'Brien, Mary (2007). The Dialectics of Reproduction. In O'Reilly, Andrea, ed., *Maternal Theory: Essential Readings*. Toronto, ON: Demeter Press. Kindle Edition, pp. 86–149.

O'Donnell, Karen (2022). *The Dark Womb*. London: SCM Press.

O'Donnell, Karen and Williams, Claire eds., (2024). *Pregnancy and Birth: Critical Theological Conceptions*. London: SCM Press. Kindle Edition.

Omotoso, Victoria Olaide (2024). Reading 1 Timothy 2.15 through the Lens of Black Pregnancy and Womanist Care. In Karen O'Donnell and Claire Williams eds., *Pregnancy and Birth: Critical Theological Conceptions*. Kindle Edition, SCM Press, pp. 75–97.

O'Reilly, Andrea ed. (2007). *Maternal Theory: Essential Readings*. Toronto, ON: Demeter Press. Kindle Edition.

Queen's University Belfast (2025). Maternal-Offspring Conflict and Cooperation During Pregnancy in Mammals, referencing D. Haig, Genetic conflict in human pregnancy. *The Quarterly Review of Biology* 68: 495–542. www.qub.ac.uk/courses/postgraduate-research/phd-opportunities/maternaloffspring-conflict-and-cooperation-during-pregnancy-in-mammals.html#.

Rahner, Karl (1974). Current Problems in Christology. *Theological Investigations*, Vol. 1. Translated by C. Ernst. London: Darton, Longman and Todd.

Raphael, Dana (1975). Matrescence, Becoming a Mother, 'A New/Old Rite of Passage'. In Dana Raphael, ed., *Being Female: Reproduction, Power and Change*. The Hague: Mouton, pp. 65–72.

Rich, Adrienne (1977). *Of Woman Born: Motherhood as Experience and Institution*. London: Virago.

Roundtable (2012). Fifty Years of Reflection on Valerie Saiving's 'The Human Situation: a Feminine View'. *Journal of Feminist Studies in Religion* 28(1): 75–133. https://dx.doi.org/10.2979/jfemistudreli.28.1.75.

Ruddick, Sara (2007). Preservative Love and Military Destruction: Some Reflections on Mothering and Peace. In Andrea O'Reilly, ed. *Maternal Theory: Essential Readings*. Bradford, Canada: Demeter Press. Kindle edition.

—— (1990). *Maternal Thinking: Towards a Politics of Peace*. London: The Women's Press.

Saiving Goldstein, Valerie (1960). The Human Situation: A Feminine View. *The Journal of Religion* 40(2): 100–112. www.jstor.org/stable/1200194.

Sear, Rebecca and Mace, Ruth (2008). Who Keeps Children Alive? A Review of the Effects of Kin on Child Survival. *Evolution and Human Behavior* 29(1): 1–18. https://doi.org/10.1016/j.evolhumbehav.2007.10.001.

Soskice, Janet Martin (1987). *Metaphor and Religious Language*. Oxford: Oxford University Press.

Spretnak, Charlene (2004). *Missing Mary: The Queen of Heaven and Her Re-Emergence in the Modern Church*. Basingstoke: Palgrave Macmillan.

Stump, Eleanore (2003). *Aquinas*. London: Routledge.

Synod of Bishops (2004). *The Eucharist: Source and Summit of the Life and Mission of the Church*. Lineamenta. XI Ordinary General Assembly, 25 February 2004. www.vatican.va/roman_curia/synod/documents/rc_synod_doc_20040528_lineamenta-xi-assembly_en.html.

Tertullian (1885). *On The Flesh of Christ*, Chapter IV. *Christian Classics Ethereal Library*. ccel.org/ccel/tertullian/christ_flesh/anf03.v.vii.iv.html.

Thomasy, Hannah (2024). A Stranger to Oneself: The Mystery of Fetal Microchimerism. *The Scientist*. www.the-scientiStcom.

Tolstoy, Leo (2012). *Anna Karenina*. Toronto, ON: Harper Perennial Classics. Kindle Edition.

Trias-Prats, Rita and Esteve, Albert (2024). Rising Female-Headed Households: Shifts in Living Arrangements or Heightened Gender Symmetry? *Population and Development Review* 51(2): 889–917. https://doi.org/10.1111/padr.12692.

Trible, Phyllis (1978). *God and the Rhetoric of Sexuality*. Philadelphia: Fortress Press.

Unicef (2025). Maternal Mortality. data.unicef.org/topic/maternal-health/maternal-mortality/.

Weil, Simone (1950). The Love of God and Affliction. *Waiting on God*. Translated by Emma Crauford. London: Fontana Books, pp. 66–76.

Wright, Wendy (2002). *Sacred Heart: Gateway to God*. London: Darton, Longman & Todd.

Wu, Katherine J. (2024). The Most Mysterious Cells in Our Bodies Don't Belong to Us. *The Atlantic*, January 3. www.theatlantic.com/science/archive/2024/01/fetal-maternal-cells-microchimerism/676996/.

Cambridge Elements

Christian Doctrine

Rachel Muers
University of Edinburgh

Rachel Muers is Professor of Divinity at the University of Edinburgh. Her publications include *Keeping God's Silence* (2004), *Living for the Future* (2008), and *Testimony: Quakerism and Theological Ethics* (2015). She is co-editor of *Ford's The Modern Theologians: An Introduction to Christian Theology Since 1918*, 4th edition (2024). She is a former president of the Society for the Study of Theology.

Ashley Cocksworth
University of Roehampton

Ashley Cocksworth is Reader in Theology and Practice at the University of Roehampton, UK. He is the author of *Karl Barth on Prayer*; *Prayer: A Guide for the Perplexed*; and (with David F. Ford) *Glorification and the Life of Faith*. His edited volumes include *T&T Clark Handbook of Christian Prayer*; *Karl Barth: Spiritual Writings*; and (with Rachel Muers), *Ford's The Modern Theologians: An Introduction to Christian Theology since 1918*.

Simeon Zahl
University of Cambridge

Simeon Zahl is Professor of Christian Theology at the University of Cambridge and a Fellow of Jesus College.

About the Series

Elements in Christian Doctrine brings creative and constructive thinking in the field of Christian doctrine to a global audience within and beyond the academy. The series demonstrates the vitality of Christian doctrine and its capacity to engage with contemporary questions.

Cambridge Elements ≡

Christian Doctrine

Elements in the Series

Life after Death after Marx
Simon Hewitt

A Theology of Home in a Time of Homelessness
Siobhán Garrigan

A Sense of the Divine: An Affective Model of General Revelation from the Reformed Tradition
N. Gray Sutanto

A Theology of Becoming: Body, Blood, Birth, and Sacrament
Tina Beattie

A full series listing is available at: www.cambridge.org/ECDR

For EU product safety concerns, contact us at Calle de José Abascal, 56–1°,
28003 Madrid, Spain or eugpsr@cambridge.org.

www.ingramcontent.com/pod-product-compliance
Lightning Source LLC
Chambersburg PA
CBHW060052120226
39575CB00016B/341